Yesterdays upon the Stairs

Jeff Barker

'Climb if you will but remember courage and strength are as naught unless accompanied by prudence, and that a momentary negligence may destroy the happiness of a life time. Do nothing in haste, look well to each step and, from the beginning, think what may be the end.'

Edward Whymper (1840-1911)
The first man to climb the Matterhorn

Published 2022 by Jeff Barker

Mill House, Cranbrook, Kent. TN17 3AH

ISBN 978-1-5272-9028-0

Printed in England by Stationery Express

3 Stone Street, Cranbrook. TN17 3HF

To Jill on the diamond anniversary of our wedding. We have walked many miles together.

Acknowledgements

I have recorded the heights of mountains and places to the best of my ability. Not all publications agree the heights of some mountains or places and, over the years, the official height of some mountains has changed, not least on Everest itself. I have sometimes taken an average of the heights gained from several publications and the web; at other times, whilst on an expedition, we have estimated our height. I readily acknowledge that I may have made mistakes in these heights and any errors are entirely mine.

The quote by Edward Whymper shown on the Tltle Page, was first seen by me at the Himalayan Institute of Mountaineering in Darjeeling. I subsequently discovered that the quote is an extract from his book 'Scrambles Amongst The Alps' first published in 1871 by John Murray, London. In particular, the last sentence of the quote provides a motto applicable to many facets of life in general. Unfortunately, to my cost, I have not always followed these wise words but now realise I should have.

I readily and thankfully acknowledge use of information gained from the following references:

'View from the Summit' by Sir Edmund Hillary published by Doubleday. Copyright Sir Edmund Hillary 1999. Reproduced here by permission of The Random House Group Ltd. This licence covers all countries except for The United States, its territories and possessions and the Philippines Republic where my book is not available..

'The Fight for Everest 1924' by E.F. Norton and other Members of the Expedition published 2015 by Vertebrate Publishing.

In the Notes to the text, pages from these publications, from which the information is gained, are identified and referenced as Hillary's Account (^Ibid 1) and Norton's Account (^Ibid 2) respectively.

I also readily and thankfully acknowledge use of the 'Report on the Lamjung Expedition' produced in 1974 by Dick Isherwood and other Members of the Expedition.

Some information is gleaned from the web and is included, with appropriate attribution, under CC BY-SA License.

The majority of photographs were taken by Jill, members of the Barker family or myself. The others, in the case of some of the Tilicho and Lamjung expeditions, by other members of those expeditions or sometimes a passer-by using my camera. Exceptionally, one photo, that of Mount Kailash, is taken from the web.

The pre-publication copy for final proof reading contained many errors and I thankfully acknowledge the contribution made by family and friends, sadly too many to mention by name, who came to my rescue with their suggestions. Thank you all.

I also thank John Montgomery and other members of staff of Stationery Express Ltd, Cranbrook, Kent for their help and advice in preparing photographs and for printing this publication.

Regarding my family, I am thankful for the great encouragement all members of my family, near and extended, have given me in my little venture on the stairs and in the recording of these memories. Many of the events I describe involve individual members of our family, sometimes all of the immediate family and sometimes a small group of us. All are happy memories and I thank my family for our many walks together. In particular I wish to thank Charlie, my grandson, for his patience and help in dealing with the many technical issues raised by me, a computer illiterate, making the hundreds of amendments and formatting the text and photographs into book form.

Lastly, I wish to thank my wife Jill for her patience in putting up with me. She has been a constant companion in virtually all of these adventures and never gives up; if she wants, she will always get to the top. Jill has saved my life on more than one occasion.

Contents

Introduction

The Idea.

Having thawed his frozen boots over the stove in order to get them on and having had breakfast, each no mean feat at an altitude of 27,900 ft, Edmond Hillary set off from Camp 9 with Norgay Tenzing. It was 6.30.a.m. on 29 May 1953; they were intent on being the first people to summit the highest peak in the world at 8848m, 29,028ft!

For much of the climb they waded through ice crusted snow, the crust breaking with every step. They took it in turns to lead. Almost at the top they were confronted with a 40 ft high rock face. Hillary led the way up via a crack between the face and an overhanging ice cornice which had separated from the face itself. Once up, Tenzing followed the same route. Both by then moving very slowly, they continued their snow climb which appeared to be never-ending. They eventually reached the summit at 11.30 a.m.[1]

Well, if they could do it then, in the bitterly freezing wind at extreme altitude, I could surely do it now, with central heating and no wind, on my stairs during lockdown. I could do it without ropes and oxygen, or indeed a chairlift, even if I am 84 and with Parkinson's.

---

[1] The first two paragraphs are paraphrases of information contained in Pages 12 to 15 of Hillary's account (^Ibid 1 refers).

Inspired by the two of them I determined to climb our house stairs to the same equivalent height. Furthermore, I would do it 'from sea level' and 'before breakfast'. I quickly decided that our ground floor level should be the 'sea level' datum and the only way I could do it 'before breakfast' would be during my early exercise session each morning. I would, however, also count any extra climbs I did during the rest of the day.

A Day of Planning and Reflection.

From our hallway at ground floor level, the house stairs rise 8'6" (2.59 m) in 13 steps at quite a steep angle. Jill, my wife, thought I should include our cellar steps but having already decided that our ground floor would be at sea level this posed problems. I would be getting my feet wet! I did reflect on the idea though and a flood of memories arose.

My first thought was of the waves lapping into Fingal's cave which we visited in 2012. We were motivated by no more than a sudden whim to see the cave which is located on Staffa, a small island not far from Iona. Jill and I arrived there after a five hundred and fifty mile car journey, a ferry and hired boat. We landed right next to the cave and walked in. We were not disappointed. The cave is staggeringly beautiful with its hexagonal basaltic columns, formed from the same ancient lava flow that resulted in the Giant's Causeway in Ireland, rising from the water, the floor of the cave washed and splashed by the never-ending waves.

Well, that's my feet wet for a start and if I went further down.... I thought of the Great Depression near Turfan, China, some 150m below sea-level, a surprise to us having, in 1987, just crossed the Tibetan Plateau, itself with an average height of 4500 m. (14,800 ft). This was getting me nowhere – I would not summit anything if I continued along that vein; the cellar steps were definitely out.

Basaltic columns at the entrance to Fingal's Cave.

As well as recording the height attained each day; I would also relate climbs of hills and mountains Jill, other members of our family and I had done or events which had happened to us at that height. Apart from the very first climb which is the lowest and was undertaken fairly recently, all other mountains and events are recorded chronologically within three main groups: UK Mountains, Mountains Elsewhere excluding the Himalayas and, lastly, Mountains in the Himalayas. In this last section there are five expeditions covered, four of them all starting from Kathmandu in Nepal and the other in Pakistan. For those starting in Nepal, the first, in 1972, was an attempt to reach Tilicho Lake, a frozen lake set high at the western end of the Annapurna massif; the second, in 1974, a first ascent of Lamjung Himal at 22, 911 ft, at the eastern end of the same massif; the third, in 1987, was a backpacking trip North East across the Himalayas, over the Tibetan plateau to Dunhuang, China, then West to Turfan, Urumchi and Kashgar and South to Peshawar in Pakistan; the fourth was a walk to Everest Base Camp in 1991. The expedition in Pakistan was a trek in the Naltar Valley, in 1989. A Land Rover trip in 2009 to Sikkim , North India and Bhutan is also included. This last section concludes with a few facts regarding the second and third highest mountains in the world, another couple of mountains to include my favourite and, lastly, Mount Everest itself.

I would start my climb on the following day, 9 November 2020, and aim to finish by Jill's eighty-second birthday in February 2021. That should allow time for a few rest days!

Yesterdays upon the Stairs

UK Mountains/Events

2020 November. Front window of House, Cranbrook, Kent.
10 ft, 3 m.

Oh, how I would have loved to have begun my attempt on Everest by saying I had climbed the Old Man of Hoy, where, I admit, I may well have started with wet feet but that is for real climbers, not for walkers like me. I will start on a more modest scale with a climb that proved more difficult than I thought; up a ladder to clamber through our narrow upstairs window to gain entry to the house when locked out. Climbing the ladder, the feet of which incidentally stood in the garden and therefore deemed by me to be below sea level, was the easy bit. Moving the heavy bedroom chair by the window and going in headfirst was a bit more difficult.

1948. Coniston Old Man, Lake District, England.
2,635 ft, 803 m.

This was the first mountain I ever climbed; I have not been up since! I climbed as a Boy Scout, aged nearly 12. We took turns to carry the pack. When I complained that my turn seemed longer than other turns, I got such a telling off I never ever again complained about carrying a load. Never again dared I suffer from attitude sickness; Jill, however, took my pack from me on one occasion when I got altitude sickness in the Himalayas and, I confess, more recently, others have offered to carry it – and I have gladly accepted.

1949 -1952. A Hill, near Trough of Bowland, England.
About 1000 ft, 300 m.

Several times over a three-year period, a school friend Terry Horsley and I would bike some 30 miles or so from Fleetwood to another friend's farmhouse at the foot of the hill. We would climb to the top where there was a very craggy plateau which extended eastwards into Yorkshire. After a descent, there would be a vegetable picking session in the garden of the farm with the daughter of the house. She kept any picked peas in her knickers; this intrigued my friend and me. Then there would be a meal before biking home.

1958. Cairngorm, Scotland.
3,742 ft. 1,141 m.

I hitchhiked to Edinburgh and, en route, as I jumped out of the cab of a lorry at Scotch Corner, a bottle of Scotch, which Jill had kindly given me, fell out of my bag and stayed in the lorry; the lorry drove off before I realised my loss. I eventually got to Edinburgh, travelling in uniform and carrying a pistol.

I stayed overnight in a B&B and hid the pistol in the double bed in my room whilst I went to a pub. Later, I returned to find my bedroom door blocked with an armchair from inside. I put my shoulder to the door which flew open to reveal two Frenchmen in the bed. They had found the pistol and were almost as terrified as I was. I quickly recovered my pistol. I slept in the single bed, also in the room, and left early the next morning.

I hitchhiked to a campsite at the foot of Cairngorm. I was on parade the next morning at 8am, along with my troop who had also hitchhiked there. All then ascended Cairngorm. In the next few days, many more mountains in the area were climbed before a halt to our running around was called in order to help the locals put out heath fires.

1979. Ben Nevis, Scotland.
4493 ft, 1370 m.

Cairngorm and Ben McDhui were again climbed by me along with Jill and our two sons Nick and Tim. The next day we travelled back via Fort William and climbed Ben Nevis, the highest mountain in UK. Avoiding a Northern or Eastern route, it is an easy climb (as we approached the bottom on our way down, we passed a man on crutches on his way up). The hardest ascent by far was to come; hours later, with our bodies stiff and aching after our long drive home, we still had to climb three flights of stairs to our flat in Edinburgh.

1993. Pen y Fan, Wales.
2,906 ft, 886 m.

Pen y Fan is the highest peak in South Wales, the highest in the country as a whole being Snowdon at 1085 m (3559 ft). We, the family, once set off for the top of Snowdon but turned back because of thunder and lightning and low cloud, the boys never really forgave me. They have subsequently been to the summit several times; I have yet to go to the top.

I have walked up Pen y Fan with Jill, and on my own, many times. Not for the first time, Jill and I walked up on the first day of 1993, a tradition which followed for some years after spending New Year's Eve at Kim and Sue Brook's house which is virtually half-way up the hillside. Kim was my best man at our wedding. The last time we climbed Pen y Fan was in April 2018 on Kim's 80th birthday. The time before that was in 2013, to take part in a church service at the summit arranged by Kim and Sue. A soldier during the SAS selection process had then recently died on the mountain and the service was held to remember him and others, including local people, who had also died in the Beacons. The service was taken by the local vicar and Kim read out a message from the Archbishop of Wales.

The Brecon Beacons is an ideal spot for the Army to get its soldiers fit, teach map-reading, build teamwork and test them. Charlie, our grandson, at one time a senior cadet himself, led a party of cadets across the Beacons on a 'Fan Dance' taking in all the local high spots.

Jill, Nick and Tim in the Cairngorms, 1979.

Charlie in the Brecon Beacons.

2005. The Pools of Dee, Larig Ghru, Scotland.
2739 ft, 835 m.

On a bright sunny day in early June, Jill and I, together with Jill's sister Jenny, her husband Chris and their daughter Anneke, walked past these pools along an ancient high-level walk, a former drove road connecting Aviemore to Braemar. The pools lie in a steep sided, scree-strewn valley with mountains on either side, Ben Macdui (4,295 ft, 1,309 m) to the East and Braeriach (4,252 ft, 1,296 m) to the West, Britain's second and third highest mountains respectively. We finished at Braemar, some 22 miles from Rothiemurchus Hut, our start point. The next day, on our 80 mile or so return journey by car, it snowed down to 1100 ft!

2008. Helm Crag, Lake District, England.
1,261 ft, 385 m.

I can't quite remember when Jill & I first climbed this beautiful little summit but it was many moons ago. Known affectionately as 'The Lion and The Lamb', it is one of our favourite walks. Having climbed it many times, we would invariably adjourn to the fireside settee in The Swan at Grasmere for a beer or G&T. On one particular Sunday, in 2008, having done the climb and had a good Swan lunch, we attended the 'Darkness to Light' service in Grasmere church.

2009. Balloon Ride, Kent, England.
900 ft, 275 m.

For one of my birthdays, Jill gave me a balloon ride. We, together with Tim, his wife Sue, their daughter Tabitha and son Charlie, took off from nearby Headcorn airfield. On this late-afternoon occasion, the weather was perfect, a lowering sun, warm and a gentle breeze. After a peaceful and calm flight, we had an exciting landing in a field of curious cows who then seemed to want to help us pack up the balloon.

We used to see lots of balloons, when we lived at Barton Stacey in Hampshire; they would fly over our house whenever the wind was from the North East providing a blue sky on a bright, but invariably cold, sunny day. The balloons looked so colourful and stately as they gently and quietly passed overhead; so much so that I was tempted to buy one. Unfortunately, I did a paper analysis of cost versus usage and it soon became clear that it would be far cheaper to hire a balloon whenever I wanted to, rather than buy. It was an analysis I would never have dreamed of doing for the sailing boat we then owned.

2010. Scafell Pike, Lake District, England.
3208 ft, 978 m.

We set off from Seathwaite without any intention of reaching the top of the Pike. The idea was merely to be on the mountain to meet Nick, Tim, Tabitha and Charlie on their way down on their self-imposed bid to climb, within twenty-four hours, Snowden, Scafell Pike and Ben Nevis, each the highest mountain in Wales, England and Scotland respectively. As it was, we didn't meet them until after we had been to the top and were nearly back at Seathwaite. They were just starting their climb. They were surprised to see us as they had thought we were still at home in Cranbrook. We chatted for only a couple of minutes and they were off again.

We later learned that they went to the top and back again in just over three hours and then immediately set off in their car for Scotland. They did not, however, do the three peaks because the weather was so bad on Ben Nevis. Subsequently they have all done the three peaks within twenty-four hours and each climbed Scafell Pike several times on its own.

2012. St Sunday Crag, Lake District, England.
2,759 ft, 841 m.

Nick and Tabitha, sometimes with Tim and Charlie, have enjoyed many walks together in the Lakes. On one occasion, they went further when they walked the Coast to Coast path from St Bees Head in the West to Robin Hood's Bay in the East, a 182-miles walk. The Crag, the highest point on their walk, provided a wonderful view of the surrounding mountains, with Helvellyn in the distance, and looked down on Ullswater Lake. Since that day, Tim painted the details of the walk on a stone and Nick and Tabitha each take it in turn to hold it for a year to remind them of their walk.

Tim and Charlie drew the short straw; they provided support for Nick and Tabitha all the way across, generally each day providing breakfast and sandwiches, packing up the camp, driving to a new campsite, erecting their tent and making the evening meal.

One notable exception to this support occurred the day before Nick and Tabitha walked the Crag. On that day, the heavens opened and it rained heavily. Jill and I walked to the top of the Honister Pass to meet them in the rain only to get further soaked as the car, driven by Tim, flashed by splashing us; not expecting us to be there, they had failed to recognise us in our wet weather gear. We immediately walked down to Seatoller House where we were staying; Nigel, the proprieter, told us that Tim had called in but had gone on to look at the site where they would be camping. In short, no one camped that night because the camp site was flooded; we arranged for everyone to stay the night at the House. When Nick and Tabitha, both very wet, eventually walked in, they were thrilled at the prospect of not going any further; hot baths, dry clothes and a good Seatoller House dinner with warm bed followed for all.

On top of Scafell Pike.

Nick and Tabitha on one of their walks.
This time to the top of Glaramara.

2012-2014. Cranbrook Church Tower, England.
75 ft, 23 m.

I volunteered to act as the church project manager for the replacement of 650 stones during the renovation of the Church Tower. My involvement lasted over two years during which I climbed the 88 steps of the Tower at least three or four times a week; those climbs alone would have taken me most of the way up Everest.

2016. Skiddaw, Lake District, England.
3,053 ft, 931 m.

Jill and I had long planned a trip to Cape Wrath with a stopover en route at our favourite watering hole, Seatoller House, in the Lakes. We would go in the September, as it happens around Nick's birthday.

I would climb Skiddaw for the first time and Jill would arrange for a man to go with me. When we got to Seatoller, Nigel welcomed us and I asked how business was; he replied that it was great. 'For example', he said, 'this weekend, we are crammed full'. 'Well, that is good.' I replied. Little did I know Jill had filled the place with family and friends for a surprise 80th birthday party for me.

We had a good weekend which included me climbing Skiddaw with 'the man' who turned out to be Nick, who had not, as he had told me, gone away for his birthday. We were accompanied by Tim, his partner Sandra, Clare, Tabitha and Charlie and other relatives. In all thirteen of us, with Jill kindly not joining us but instead looking after my 86-year-old sister, Joan, who had also turned up. After our weekend, Jill and I went on to Cape Wrath.

Years before, in 1954, I set off to climb Skiddaw with Joan and her husband Jim. Having eaten our sandwiches early on and not on a recognised path, we gave up in thick cloud, rain, thunder and lightning.

Jill and I set out again in 2017 on my 81st birthday but we decided, in the thick cloud and strong wind, having done the hard bit and reached the foot of Little Man, to return to the car park below.

2016. Cape Wrath, Scotland.
About 800 ft, 250 m.

Cape Wrath lies at the most North-Westerly point of the British mainland. The sea cliffs in the area are the highest on the mainland. At the Cape, there stands a lighthouse built in 1823 by Robert Stephenson. The access road, which runs through a military live bombing range, was built at the same time and connects to a weather-dependent small passenger ferry which is required to cross Loch Durness.

One can only visit the Cape when the weather is good and there is no live firing. Such was the day when Jill and I visited a couple of days after my 80th birthday party at Seatoller.

We had also gone to Sutherland to see, at nearby Tongue, if a small footbridge which I had arranged to be built in 1979 was still there. It was but, rather like the proverbial axe, had recently had new timber decking and handrails. The bridge was built as training for the Army, one of many engineering projects undertaken as Military Aid to the Civil Community

2017. Helvellyn, Lake District, England.
3,116 ft, 950 m.

I climbed this mountain with Nick and Tabitha. They took pity on what they rightly considered to be an old man and offered to carry my pack; I was delighted to accept their kind offer. We reached the top via Swirral Edge but came back the easy route via Lower Man, skirted Keppel Cove and down to Glenridding where Jill met us.

Celebrating my 80th Birthday on top of Skiddaw. I took the photograph!
Left to Right: Tabitha, David Odell, Nick, Jennifer Deverell, Sue Stitt, Tim,
Charlie, Chris Deverell, Sandra, Clare, Chris Stitt, Virginia Odell.

Joan and I on Skiddaw in 1954.

Lighthouse at Cape Wrath.

Foot Bridge at Tongue – built by the Army as military aid to the civil community.

2020. Cranbrook Windmill, England.
72 ft, 22 m.

Jill and I watched from our house, Mill House, as a mobile crane and cherry picker, the biggest in both cases either of us had ever seen, removed the sweeps (sails) from the Windmill prior to renovation. The Mill, the tallest smock mill in the South of England, now looks a bit sad without its whirling arms.

2021. South West Coastal Path, England.
128,280 ft, 39,110 m.

Having returned with Sandra from a month-long 'training camp' in Tenerife, where many miles were either cycled or walked by them, Tim took part, again as a chaperone, in the Land's End to John O'Groats cycle ride; that is until he reached Edinburgh where, along with over three hundred other cyclists, he fell victim to a non-covid virus and had to retire.

A fortnight later Tim and Sandra set out from Minehead, Devon, on what turned out to be a walk of 47 days covering 710 miles, including the distance to and from the path from the B&B's, pubs or hotels where they stayed overnight. They were joined on different days by various friends and relatives including Charlie (twice), Nick, Clare, Tabitha, Hannah and Jill and me. On November 4 we met them at Poole, Dorset, the end of the path, with much flag waving and champagne. En route, they had walked a seemingly endless number of small hills which together totalled a height of 39,110 metres, the equivalent of nearly four and half Everests. That I think puts my little effort on the stairs into perspective.

Cranbrook Mill at work.

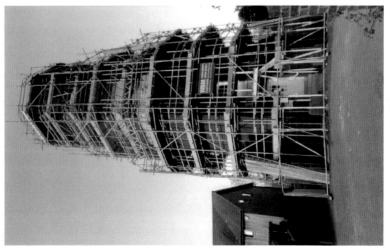

Sweeps removed and Mill ready to be painted.

Yesterdays upon the Stairs

Mountains/Events Elsewhere excluding the Himalayas

1959. Norway. Parachuting Height over Bardufoss Dropping Zone.
About 1000 ft, 305 m.

On a parachute exercise inside the Arctic Circle, we took off not far from a village called Hell and were dropped onto a snow-covered bog. Our red berets and parachute smocks were no match for the wet and cold! We spent a week 'fighting' the Norwegians who, despite the snow, seemed to contour their way round the mountains on their bikes or skis, whilst we climbed up and down them. 2-1 to the Norwegians, I reckon. Then, as if by magic, I, together with Kim who was also on the exercise, were withdrawn early to go up to Cambridge. We had gone from Hell to Heaven!

1961. Yellowstone National Park, Wyoming, USA.
8,410 ft, 2,564 m.

For our honeymoon in 1961, Jill and I drove across the States. We had arrived in New York with a £100 to last three months. After the first night, staying in Flushing Meadows which cost £10, we realised we must move on quickly to the Okanagan Valley in the far West of Canada where we were guaranteed work, fruit picking. We 'Greyhound-bussed' overnight to Akron, Ohio where we stayed with my old school- and biking-friend, Terry Horsley, then a doctor. He and his wife were, amazingly, about to emigrate to the Okanagan Valley; we would accompany them there by car. The next day, Terry came home to say he had a car, a Ford shooting brake, for us to drive across; a doctor friend of his wanted the car driven across and sold in the West, cars selling there for far higher prices than in the East where they were manufactured. We all set off in two cars, initially roughly in convoy but that sometimes proved inconvenient. We camped overnight wherever we ended up.

All went well until the Badlands in South Dakota where, in the first rains for some time making the road 'slick', I turned the car over. 'Get out' I said to Jill, thinking the car might catch fire. 'It's pouring!' protested Jill. Fortunately, a police car came along and took us off to Rapid City where we arranged recovery and repair. After a few days we picked the car up, driveable but somewhat battered and with no rear window but, more significantly, with new tyres to replace the threadbare ones which had contributed to the accident.

We motored on, sleeping in the back of the car overnight but ever mindful of wildlife with our absent rear window, particularly the bears in Yellowstone Park in the Rockies. In the Park we did see some bears and other wild life by day but none ever bothered us. We also witnessed 'Old Faithful' the geyser which 'blows' regularly, sending a fountain high into the air. We continued north-westwards until we reached about 70 miles beyond Spokane, Washington State. There we crossed the

Grand Coulee Dam on the Columbia River, an impressive feat of engineering, about a mile wide and over four hundred feet high. We then travelled northwards; crossed the Canadian border (where we were a bit surprised by having to pay customs duty on our new American tyres) and eventually reached the Okanagon Lake. We stayed with Joan and Terry in their new home and duly got our job, picking fruit.

Picking fruit proved hard work. Fruit varied from apples, including extra fancy which required, before picking, judgement of a specific percentage of redness, pears, apricots and, the hardest to pick of all, sour cherries, seemingly millions required to fill a large box. Picking the latter Jill got sunstroke. We worked alongside professional pickers, itinerant Canadian-Japanese, who could put a ladder against a tree from which they could invariably pick the whole tree. Despite us requiring three or four ladder positions to achieve the same and, despite never realising whether we were picking by the box or the hour, we picked sufficient fruit for us to be able to pay our way with Terry and save some for travelling.

When not picking fruit, we did a few local trips around the area and on one occasion I drove to Lillooet crossing Pavilion Mountain (2,939 m, 6,688 ft), a hair-raising experience on a rough track which left me with a migraine when we got there. Lillooet was a gold mining town; the beginning of the trail during the Cariboo Gold Rush and, around 1860, the most populated town, apart from San Francisco, west of Chicago. On the same trip we had, of course, to visit Barkerville, another former gold mining town nearby. From what we remember the place was virtually deserted.

We earned enough from our fruit picking to get us back to New York. Indeed, we picked sufficient fruit for us to afford a visit to Victoria on the Island, Vancouver and train to Calgary, where, having received a surprise telegram on the train to get off there, we stayed with new found friends. We trained to Toronto where we visited Niagara Falls and bussed to New York. We arrived with less than a dollar in our pockets; this had to last the next 12 hours before our flight back home.

We saw in a bookshop 'How to live on a dollar a day in New York'. We went in, thumbed through it but could not buy; subsequently, as recommended in the book, we visited Central Park, the Empire State building and various museums and exhibitions, all free. Fortunately also, finding a cheaper than expected way of getting to the Airport, we found we could afford to buy two doughnuts!

We boarded our charter plane and, although we had all paid the same fare, Jill, because all women were given this privilege, travelled first class and, because Jill had a husband, I was allowed to sit with her. 'Wake me up', said Jill, 'when the food and drink come'. I duly woke her as soon as the Champagne arrived.

Twenty-five years later we returned to the very spot where we had picked fruit but, by then, the fruit trees which had swept down to the Okanagan Lake were no longer there. In their place stood the grounds of a large house and in those grounds stood a hot tub in which we drank cocktails with the owner of the former orchard. Jill and I preferred the orchard!

1964. Mont Blanc, French/Italian Border.
15,770 ft, 4,808 m.

Mont Blanc is the highest mountain in Western Europe and was first climbed towards the end of the eighteenth century, almost a century before mountaineering as a hobby took off. This is another mountain we have not climbed. However, one Edmund Clark did; his grave is in the churchyard of St Dunstan's, our church in Cranbrook, Kent and therefore warrants inclusion here. The engraving on the grave records:

'In memory of Edmund Clark MD, one of the few enterprising travellers who have succeeded in ascending the summit of Mont Blanc. He was the only son of Mr John Clark and Elizabeth, his wife, and departed this life on March 26th 1837 aged 37'.

Well done Edmund!

Robin Jordan, a close friend of ours, also climbed Mont Blanc in 1964. We saw Robin just before he died a couple of years ago; he was in hospital and not at all well, his illness aggravated by dementia. He recognised us immediately, however, and, in chatting, we teased him about the time he ran up and down the stairs with a heavy rucksack full of stones practising for his ascent of Mont Blanc. With that his eyes lit up and, clear as a bell, he told us of how excited and joyful he was at reaching the summit; he described in some detail the magnificent views which had spread out before him on a glorious sunny day.

Jill on our way to Lillooet, the Fraser River below.

Mont Blanc taken from high up Meribel Valley area, French Alps.

1973. Slopes of Sunset Peak, Lantau Island, Hong Kong.
2100 ft, 640 m.

Camping overnight on the slopes of Sunset Peak (2850 ft) with Nick and Tim, I got out in the middle of the night to go to the loo. In a clear sky, I was amazed to see the Comet Kohoutek with its trail of light passing overhead. I woke the boys to witness the spectacle. Apparently, Kohoutek's last appearance was 150,000 years ago with its next appearance due after 75,000 years. We probably won't see it again!

1977. Thompson's Falls, Kenya.
3116 ft, 950 m.

I, along with two others, started a reconnaissance for a new road at the Falls. The proposed road was to link the Falls to Lake Baringo, down the mountains and across the Laikipia Plateau to the West. The reconnaissance was done on foot and took three days through the bush. We carried all our tents, food, water and equipment between us. Ever conscious of the wild life, I entered a dried wadi on one occasion and was startled, to say the least, by a number of warthogs who seemed very angry and made much noise at being disturbed. Fortunately, that was our only near encounter with wildlife.

1977 and 1992. Kilimanjaro, Tanzania.
19,342 ft, 5,895 m.

This is the highest free-standing mountain in the world. There is a magnificent view from Amboseli Game Reserve where we were staying in 1976 on our drive round Kenya in an old Land Rover which seemingly consumed more oil than petrol. If we could not find more substantial shelter, we camped; the only trouble with the latter being the monkeys, or worse the baboons, for whom we provided an irresistible curiosity. On this occasion we stayed in a thatched hut, accommodation forming part of a game lodge.

The hut was complete with resident vampire bat and battered exercise book for visitor's comments. 'If you want the comforts of home, I say, stay at home' was one of the comments. A previous visitor had also commented 'How beautiful is the view of Kilimanjaro'. 'Indeed, it is' commented Nick, adding 'but the problem is I hate my father'; father being cross with him for not helping to unload the Land Rover. Tim entered our address in UK. A few years later a friend of ours, Jungly Drake, stayed in the same hut; he saw Nick's comment and added 'I know his dad and I agree with every word Nick has said!'

Fifteen years later, Nick and Tim were climbing Kilimanjaro together, with others and three guides. They reached the final hut, still well over two hours walk from the summit where they were to spend the night. During the night Nick thought that Tim was behaving strangely and talking nonsense; he recognised the symptoms of altitude sickness and informed the guides who were in another hut. They agreed that Tim should go down immediately and this was quickly arranged with one of the guides to accompany him. The next morning Nick went on to the summit and later, when asked his name to go on the certificate confirming that he had got to the top, he said his name was Tim. The same day he descended to a lower hut where he expected to meet Tim but in fact Tim had gone down even further. They caught up with each other two days later.

Nick and Tim then flew on to Cairo. Jill and I knew they would be there then and thought we would fly out to surprise them. We went with Tim's girlfriend, Rebecca Hill, who had arranged to meet Tim, in the bar of a particular hotel. When we got to the hotel there was of course more than one bar. Rebecca toured the bars and eventually found Nick and Tim firmly ensconced. It took all her persuasive powers to get them to move bars to meet 'these interesting people' she had met on the flight out.

1986. 'The Edge of the World', Riyadh, Saudi Arabia.
2,010 ft, 612 m.

Jill and I lived in Riyadh, the capital, for a couple of years where, I confess, my job was not particularly demanding; Jill and I were therefore able to spend a lot of time in the desert. A favourite camping spot was at 'The edge of the world', a cliff edge on a lengthy fault line which dropped, almost sheer, at least 400 ft or more, several miles out of Riyadh. Jill and I had a tent made for us in the local market, a beautiful tent of yellow, maroon and blue stripes inside and white canvas on the outside. I thought I had given very detailed specifications for it but was disappointed, when we picked it up, that I had not specified the stripes should be vertical. I mistakenly thought that this was obvious. Anyway, this horizontal-striped tent has served us very well since and it is still used to this day in UK for summer parties. We christened it on Christmas Day 1986 at 'The edge of the world'.

The near vertical fault line provides an exciting viewpoint of the desert below and had, near Riyadh, a fairly steep camel trail up it. The trail that, according to legend, Abdul Aziz had ascended with a small camel force to capture Dir'aiyah, the mud city capital of the emirate, which ultimately led to the takeover by him of the throne of Saudi Arabia. This camel trail proved an exceptionally good walk, a favourite for the many UK visitors we were required to look after. On one occasion, Jill and I took a particular VIP up it. We set off very early in the morning, before the sun became too hot, starting in the red sands below. We slowly wound our way up and, round one bend in the track near the top, our visitor, by now beginning to feel the heat, was delighted and surprised to see our tent set up with chairs etc and breakfast for us about to be served.

1987. Huayna Picchu, Peru.
8,833 ft, 2,693 m.

Travelling on public transport, we visited a number of towns, including Cusco and Quito; the most abiding memory of our visit is that of the Inca stonework which defies explanation of how it is achieved. There appears to be no mortar between the stones, all of which are extra-large. Irrespective of the shape of the joint, it is impossible at any point to slide even a credit card between the stones. We also had a flight in a light aircraft over the Nazca lines to view the ancient lines on the ground which, unrecognisable from the ground, traced the outline of various birds and animals. A message to the Gods?

We also visited Machu Pichu, the fifteenth century city of the Incas and, whilst there, climbed the 850 ft prominence of Huayna Picchu which dominates the deserted city. On the way up Jill was not at all well but, after a short rest, she insisted we continue to the top which we did.

Woman with Llama by magnificent stonework.

Huayna Picchu.

1987. Lake Titicaca, Peru.
12,507 ft, 3812 m.

Lake Titicaca is generally acknowledged to be the highest navigable lake in the world. Jill and I had a day trip on the lake. We saw many local indigenous people living on islands they had made from the reeds found in the shallows; on the thick reed-rafts they had reed houses and market stalls, full of fruit, vegetables grown locally ashore, and fish. All their boats were similarly fashioned out of the reeds. This ancient method of boatbuilding was used to build Thor Heyerdahl's reed raft which, on his Kon-Tiki expedition in 1947, successfully made it across the Pacific Ocean, by drifting with the current to Polynesia showing that as a possible ancient migration route.

1987. La Paz, Bolivia.
11,946 ft, 3642 m.

When China took control of Tibet, its capital city, Lhasa, could no longer claim to be the highest capital in the world. That title passed to La Paz with an altitude of only 14 metres lower. Those 14 metres were not sufficient though to eradicate the effects of altitude on visitors to the city. We were travelling by train across the altiplano to La Paz when the train stopped at a station even before reaching that city. I got out of the train to get a cup of tea but the tea trolley was at the other end of the platform. I ran the length of the station and, when I got to the trolley, I realised I was wholly out of breath; the effects of altitude had become apparent even before we reached Le Paz. We had our tea though.

When we got to La Paz, we did some walking in the snow-covered surrounding hills but took it gently and there was no further ill effect. At La Paz, we celebrated the fact that, at last, we had become multi millionaires; but in pesos, with a cup of coffee costing one and half million pesos.

1988. Mada'in Salih, Saudi Arabia.
2,545 ft, 776 m.

Having driven from Riyadh in three Range Rovers, we, a small party including Jill and Nick, camped in the desert outside Mada'in Salih. Two thousand years ago and like its sister city of Petra, Mada'in Salih formed part of the Nabatean Empire. In 1988 it was recognised, at least by one or two ex-pats lucky enough to get permission to go there, as the start point for any visit to the many rock monoliths, all with beautifully carved facades, forming now deserted tombs.

Whilst we visited some of the monoliths, more significantly for me, Mada'in Salih also provided ready access to part of the old Turkish railway line, built in the early 20th Century. The line connected Damascus to Medina and Mecca. The line is no longer working and hasn't since Lawrence of Arabia blew it up; as an Arab speaking British Army officer, on his initiative, he was sent to galvanize and support the Arab Revolt against the Turks during the First World War. The iron rails have disappeared but the trains are, or were in 1988, all derailed and either standing or lying on their side in the otherwise empty desert. All trains are wind- and sand-blasted but otherwise well preserved by the extremely dry heat.

We drove on a track parallel to the line; the line itself, still with its ballast intact, not trafficable because most of the culverts had disappeared. Precisely at every eleven-kilometre interval, there was a station, The building was more like a small fort to house the Turkish soldiers who then guarded the line. These forts were also relatively well preserved with spare ballast beautifully laid out as though it had been put there yesterday. There was the occasional water point but no water.

We drove southwards alongside the track for 80 miles or so before literally coming up against a painted brick wall, the end of the line. We were on the outskirts of Medina by then and, at a sign which displayed a large arrow and stated 'Infidels turn off', duly followed the arrow. We headed for Jeddah on the coast where we stayed the night with friends before driving the six hundred miles across the desert back home to Riyadh.

As an aside, in 1925 my father, along with several others, shared a billet with Lawrence at Bovington Camp, Dorset. Lawrence, who then as Trooper Shaw, was hiding from the inevitable limelight which his exploits attracted. My father said Lawrence kept very much to himself.

1988. Fraser's Hill, Malaysia.
4777 ft, 1,456 m.

I played my second ever, and thankfully last, round of golf on the course at Fraser's Hill. All I remember was that it was a gloriously sunny day, not too hot, the course was empty and Tim and I had a lovely walk looking for my golf balls; I don't think I won. Nick was with Jill.

We had all met several days before at the E&O Hotel in Penang, a meeting arranged the month before with Nick in Saudi and Jill and I had not seen or had contact with the boys since then; they were on their own walkabouts. Jill and I had travelled by train from Bangkok, stayed with our friends the Corsellis' in Kuala Lumpur, bussed and ferried to Penang and were travelling with Nick and Tim to the East coast by car, with a stopover at Fraser's Hill, for a week's holiday together.

A tomb from the Nabatean days.

Train damaged during the Arab Revolt.

1994. Horten's Plain, Sri Lanka.
About 7,200 ft, 2,200 m.

Jill and I visited Sri Lanka for three weeks in 1994. We did all the touristy things, backpacking our way around but staying in reasonable accommodation; in the Galle Face Hotel on arrival in Columbo.

In Kandy, we stayed for a few days in an Art Deco bungalow with a wonderful garden, full of flowers and colourful butterflies. I sat in the garden, with swollen feet after our flight, and spent two days completing an application form for a job in Ghana which Jill had found me. With no photograph available to attach to the application, I described myself instead. We got waylaid by a local on the way to post the application; he said he was an airline pilot and going to London the next day; he would post it in London. I gave it to him to post. Jill said I was mad! The upshot of this, when I enquired on return two weeks later, was that the form had not been received. I gave up the idea of the job. A fortnight after that, the employer telephoned to say they had just received the application form. Two interviews later, I got the job – a countrywide adult literacy project.

We eventually left Kandy, with my feet restored to normal size. We went on to Sigiriya and climbed the rock to the small plateau on top; thence, via Dambola to see the cave paintings, to Nuwara Eliya. There we had (school) dinner, complete in jacket and tie taken especially for the occasion, at the Hill Club. We then went on to Horten's Plain and stayed at the Farr Inn, an old hunting lodge. Next morning, very early before breakfast, we went into the bush to view the local Sambar deer, renowned for their long antlers; it was a gorgeously beautiful sunny morning.

We then caught a very slow train, essentially a goods train with one carriage for passengers where, because the carriage was crowded, we sat by an open door and watched the countryside go by. It cost the equivalent of 11p for those three marvellous hours.

We alighted at Ella where we allowed ourselves to be hijacked by a local boy who took us to his family house which, as promised, did indeed provide excellent accommodation. The local boy, aged about seventeen, considered himself to be an expert on elephants and reckoned he understood them. We let him, armed only with a large knife, take us into the bush, the three of us on foot, to see wild elephants. We approached to within 20 yards of a small herd, too close for me!

We returned to Columbo by ancient bus which broke down twice on the way. We finished our stay in Sri Lanka at the delightful Mount Lavinia Hotel overlooking the sea before flying home.

1995-1996. Wli Falls, Volta Region, Ghana.
2904 ft, 885 m.

Mount Afida, the highest mountain in Ghana, is another mountain we have not climbed. (There are so many mountains we have not climbed!) We lived in Ghana for three years and many times Jill and I visited the nearby Wli falls in those mountains. The falls are the highest in West Africa. In 1996, this entailed an hour long walk through the tropical forest, over streams and fallen tree trunks, to the foot of the falls.

Wli Falls, locally pronounced Vlee, were affectionally known, by us in our 'ex-pat' way, as the Willy Falls. A quite spectacular sight with a vertical drop of 80m. Also spectacular was the sight of so many fruit bats clinging upside down to the cliffs or as they soared, en masse, such that the sky darkened above us. We took Jenny and Chris there and Kim and Sue, among others.

Jill at the 'Willy' Falls, Ghana.

2005. The Heaney Glacier, Island of South Georgia.
3,100 ft. 950m.

We were at anchor in a bay just off the island of South Georgia. Mount Paget, the highest peak on the island, was on the skyline; much closer and flowing into the bay was a glacier, the Heaney Glacier, the central feature of a little sketch I was making. Standing nearby was Jill with John Heaney, after whom the Glacier was named, following his survey of the glacier some fifty or more years earlier. John kindly added his signature to my picture.

The Island of South Georgia is one of the most dramatic and beautiful places to which Jill and I have ever been. The mountainous interior snow bedecked and the rugged coast line standing defiantly on the West coast against the constant onslaught of the waves of the roaring Scotia Seas. The surrounding sea, sailed over by the wandering albatross and other birds, is alive with Krill, other fish life, penguins, seals of many varieties and whales. Nearby we visited a beach with over ten thousand King penguins – and I was bigger than all of them! Nevertheless, inquisitive and confident young brown fluffy penguins, clearly in charge, examined me as one would a man from outer space.

The island was, of course, home to a now virtually deserted whaling station at Grytvicken. The station's large whale oil tanks, ships and deserted buildings, rusty and dilapidated, are now home only to hundreds of seals. There are, however, still a well-maintained Norwegian church, a post office and the grave of 'The Boss', Sir Ernest Shackleton. A small number of British Antarctic Survey researchers temporarily also live there.

The Heaney Glacier, South Georgia.

King Penguin beach, South Georgia.

Beached whaleboat at Grytvicken, South Georgia.

Abandoned whale oil tanks with sleeping seal, South Georgia.

2005. Point Wild, Elephant Island, Antarctica.
About 400 ft, 122 m.

Although we did not climb this point, Jill and I, as members of the James Caird Society, cannot afford to ignore it. We were in a RIB trying to land on Elephant Island but it was too windy and the sea at the shoreline was too rough; we could only get about 25 metres from the shore.

Point Wild is a bleak inhospitable wind-swept narrow strip of land culminating in the Point itself. We had wanted to visit the site on the shore where Frank Wild, in 1916, had lived with 21 other members of the Trans-Antarctic expedition for over 4 months whilst 'The Boss', Ernest Shackleton, set off in a small boat, James Caird, to seek help. Shackleton eventually rescued all his men without loss of life. He returned after an epic, 800 miles, sail to South Georgia, the nearest approachable land, thence by bigger boat to South America where he arranged a Chilean rescue ship.

Those rescued had originally called the bluff 'Cape Wild' but a sense of proportion by the Committee for Antarctic Names, no doubt meeting in surroundings far removed from Elephant Island, decided that the name of Point Wild was more appropriate.

Jill in RIB approaching Point Wild.

2005. Mount Teide, Tenerife, Canary Islands.
12,188 ft, 3,715 m.

All of the immediate Barker clan, generally in pairs at different times, have visited the Canary Islands several times. In 2005 Jill and I watched Tim and two of his fireman friends participate in an Ironman event in Lanzarote. However, recent trips have mainly been to either Tenerife or La Gomera. Both islands provide ideal walking and, if you enjoy biking uphill, there are plenty of challenging cycle rides too.

Nick, in particular, often goes regularly in January until sometime in March to escape the cold, damp winters of Cambridge. He has criss-crossed the hills of these two islands several times; he knows the coastal walks and the tops of most hills.

Whenever Clare has joined Nick, Jill and I have gone out too for a few days and the four of us have walked the hills. Two memorable occasions stand out, both on La Gomera. On the first, we went to the top of the central peak, Alto de Garojonay at 1,484 m (4,877 ft), where the trees were all blackened and burnt from a fire which had devastated a very large area several months earlier. The second was when Jill had a spectacular fall, her roll down the rocky mountainside only stopped by a prickly pear bush. Quite apart from the effects of the prickly spikes, she sustained injuries to her ribs, back and foot which took several months to heal.

From several vantage points on La Gomera, there are good views of Mount Teide across the sea, on Tenerife. Nick has walked to the top of that mountain several times. On each occasion he has necessarily been required to book his visit via the refuge hut, still about an hour and a half's walk from the summit; the idea being to leave very early in the morning to be on top at sunrise. It is always cold on top, with permanent ice, and windy. On each occasion he has descended a different route; one time, with Tim and Sandra, they descended via the 'old' original volcanic peak, a five hour walk to where they had left their car.

Mount Teide from La Gomera, Canary Isles.

Montana Roja.

2018. Ootacomund, India.
8154 ft, 2486 m.

With a letter of introduction sent from UK a month beforehand, Jill and I visited the 'Ooty' Club. The gardens were beautifully kept and the brass work at the entrance to the club gleamed. Otherwise, the club itself was disappointing mainly because the club was, at the time, virtually deserted of members; there were just a few members of staff who did not appear to be particularly helpful or welcoming. We did manage to get gin and tonics and then left soon afterwards but not until we had explored the empty rooms, most with nostalgic pictures of 'dear old England' on the walls, and had seen the original snooker table on which the game was invented.

2019 and 2020. Montana Roja, near El Medano, Tenerife.
561 ft, 171 m.

A red rock extinct volcano with fantastic views out to sea provides a perfect platform from which to watch the kite surfers in action with their colourful kites criss-crossing the sky. This little mountain was climbed by Jill, by way of celebration of her 80th and 81st birthdays, accompanied on each occasion by Nick and Clare, Tim and Sandra and me. Tabitha & Charlie also did the climb on the first occasion; they had flown out for the weekend to Jill's complete surprise. Jill did not feel well on the day of her 80th birthday but managed the climb the day after.

2020. La Marmotte, France.
15,988 ft, 4,873 m.

Tim has this idea that he must periodically enter an extreme event to test his fitness. He has therefore completed a number of Iron Man events in this country and elsewhere; he also did the Marathon des Sables. He has participated in the Land's End to John O'Groats cycle ride, once with Sandra, once as a cycling bike mechanic and once as a cycling chaperone. His latest venture was the cycling event, La Marmotte, this entails a 175 km circuit in the French Alps ending up near the start. During the event his average speed was 18 km per hour, he ascended 15,998 ft in the 9 hrs 43 minutes it took him to complete the circuit. So far it has taken me 61 days to reach this height. He is fit!

Yesterdays upon the Stairs

Himalayan Mountains/Events

1972. Tilicho Lake Expedition, Nepal.

Kathmandu.
About 4,500 ft, 1,372 m.

Jill and I first went to Kathmandu in 1972, a few years after it was acknowledged in the sixties to be the end of the hippie trail. As a reminder of those days there were still a few Hashish shops around. The city was a quiet and peaceful place with no paper litter; street food was served on banana leaves which, if thrown away, were eaten by the holy cows which were everywhere.

The streets, with their many temples, were thronged with people and the odd load-carrying camel or elephant and there were very few cars. Wide streets were used to lay out the wheat and other harvests for threshing and drying and, particularly on the outskirts, washing was laid out to dry on the ground and bushes.

Over the years we have visited Kathmandu a number of times and, after each subsequent year, the city, the vehicular traffic, the pollution and litter had increased; only the number of cows seemed to have decreased but some are still about. Incidentally, and unfortunately for Jill it was more than incidental, on one visit, a holy cow butted her on her coccyx which remained painful for about a year.

51

Hashish Shop, Kathmandu. 1972.

Morning wash and garland seller, Kathmandu. 1972.

Harvest time in the centre of Kathmandu. 1972.

Typical Fruit shop, Kathmandu. 1972.

Kathmandu, being the capital, provides the necessary start point for most expeditions or treks. I spent hours with the Customs retrieving our equipment and only succeeded after completing six handwritten copies of seemingly every form imaginable. Similarly, I waited several hours at one Ministry to obtain the required trekking permits. We visited the British Embassy and confirmed our use of the Pension Paying Post at Pokhara as a base before setting off on our approach march.

I arranged transport for our equipment to be taken to Pokhara. The road to Pokhara had been closed for some months due to landslides and there was doubt that it would be open. Jill fortuitously met the manager of the Fishtail Lodge Hotel in Pokhara who had just driven one of the first vehicles to get through; his name was Fred Barker, a Swiss/Argentinian. He offered to drive Jill to Pokhara which she gladly accepted. Fred was a larger-than-life character and took great pleasure, when stopped at the many road checkpoints, to declare his name and introduce Jill as Mrs Barker but then, to complicate matters unnecessarily, adding laughingly 'We are not married.' I set off for Pokhara before them, by lorry with our expedition equipment, but they soon overtook me.

Washing in the early morning mist, Kathmandu 1972.

Pokhara.
About 3,000 ft, 915 m.

The Gurkha Pension Paying Post at Pokhara proved ideal as a start point, with accommodation for all expedition members and space for sorting out our food, climbing gear and equipment. It was all prioritized and numbered into loads, each generally about 25 to 30 kg; the loads to be carried by porters were put into baskets traditionally slung on their backs from a band round their foreheads.

A Head Porter, a cook and twenty-six porters were hired and paid for the first few days; each porter was given a sweater.

On a day in early October we started our approach march. We walked through Pokhara, each house especially clean and decorated with banana leaves, red cloth and shining brass pots for, that very day, the king was due to visit.

Ulleri.
About 6,625 ft, 2020 m.

This village, where we stayed on the second night of our approach march, is included for two reasons. Like many hill villages it has steps leading up to it, but few could be as long or as steep as those leading to Ulleri; certainly, they are the longest and steepest we have ever encountered on all our travels in the Himalayas. We did not count the steps but there are reputed to be well over 3,200.

The second reason is that Jill has this vision of about ten little Jeffs, all in single file, climbing up those steps. This expedition had provided me with the ideal opportunity to get rid of about ten different coloured sweaters, from pea green to cinnamon, which my mother had over the years kindly knitted me. I did not like the colours and the jumpers were invariably too small for me; they fitted the porters perfectly.

The Pension Paying Post in Pokhara. 1972.
About to start approach march to base camp.

Pokhara ready to welcome the King. 1972.

Tatopani.
About 4750 ft, 1450 m.

This stopover, 4 days walk from Pokhara, has to be included in this Tilicho story because it provided our first sight of the Kali Gandaki river which we were to follow up to Johmson, the northern limit to which we were authorised to trek. The river was ice cold, despite apparently 'boiling' its way South, down the 'deepest valley in the world'. To the West, the Daulghiri range ascends to 26,810 ft and, to the East, the Nilgiri and Annapurna Ranges ascend respectively 25,064 ft and 26,504 ft.

Tatopani also has to be included for two other notable reasons. Tatopani, true to its name, provided us with our first decent wash since setting out, a bathe in the naturally occurring hot water pools there.

The other reason provided us with much mirth at the expense of one of our team. Unlike everyone else in the Team, one member, who will remain nameless, was particularly fed up with the 'endless rice and dahl meals' we had had. It was agreed that, as it was his birthday, we would break open the Army rations we had with us and he could choose what we ate. Leaving him to brief the cook we all went to the hot springs to bathe. Joining us there later, the member told us that we would start with tinned salmon; this would be followed by Scotch Mutton Style, ending with tinned treacle pudding. As it turned out we had all those ingredients but unfortunately mixed all together; the cook had emptied all the tins into one big pot and heated them; the birthday-boy was not amused but we were.

Marpha.
About 8,850 ft, 2,700 m.

We arrived in Marpha, 5 days from Pokhara on the day of what should have been an auspicious occasion for the village. The King was due to helicopter to the village, in particular to visit the horticultural research station there but the bitterly cold winds, which regularly every morning sweep the valley northwards for several hours and then southwards for several more, proved too strong and the helicopter could not make it.

Fortunately for us, Jill and I happened to be passing the house of the manager of the research station, Pasang Sherpa, at that moment and he kindly invited us in to share the meal planned for the king; goat, a rare treat, rice, dahl and chopped cabbage. We sat with Pasang and a few other males, the women and children almost out of sight. Jill was very conscious of their absence and determined not to eat too much goat to save it for them. Pasang Sherpa was well educated; he could speak English and French fluently and converse in several other languages. He had accompanied Dr Snelgrove, of the School of Oriental Studies, on his Himalayan journey around the East of Nepal, returned to UK with him, and again accompanied him on his Himalayan Pilgrimage around the West of the country. He features strongly in Snelgrove's book of the same name.[2]

Late in the afternoon we left the research station, leaving behind many thanks for such a pleasant, generous and enjoyable lunch. Little did Jill know then that she would later return to the station where she would live with the family for ten days, get to know them quite well and understand fully why the village is called Marpha, meaning 'hard working people'.

---

[2] Himalayan Pilgrimage' by David Snellgrove is 'a study of Tibetan religion by a traveller though Western Nepal', published 1961 by Bruno Cassirer (Publishers) Ltd.

Johmsom.
9000 ft. 2,750 m.

The next day Jill and I walked to Johmsom, for once, relatively along the flat. It was a sunny day and the strong early morning Southerly cold wind blew us on our way. We passed several cheerful women outside their homes either carpet making or spinning wool. As we approached Johmson the first evidence of the settlement was a crashed aircraft on a nearby airstrip; we understand that the aircraft had sat there for some time and the small airport was closed. We visited the doctor's surgery, a stone walled hut with no apparent medical facilities; it had a purpose-built hole in the roof through which the sun shone brightly over the 'operating table'. The hole somehow kept out the cold wind, the cause of so many respiratory illnesses suffered by the locals.

Johmsom was, in 1972, six days walk from Pokhara. It now has a new road linking it to Pokhara so can be reached by car easily within a long day's drive; also, there are now many hotels along the way. The airfield is back in operation and is an hour's flight from Pohkara. Also in 1972, with Tibet closed to foreigners, Johmsom was the northern limit to which foreigners could trek. The Mustang Region which lay to the North and the track eventually eastwards to Mukintath, a holy city for Buddhists and Hindus, which led to the pass, Thorung La, at 17,800 ft, 5427 m, were all forbidden territory. Nowadays that route eastwards which circles the Annapurna massif, going down the Marsyandi Khola from the Thorung La, is open. Our trek permits were duly stamped by the soldiers on duty at Johmsom.

We retraced our steps southwards, again with the strong wind behind us, it having changed direction at midday. A new camp for the night had been set up at Syang, roughly midway between Johmsom and Marpha. We were then only a half day's walk from our proposed base camp area to the East.

Base Camp.
About 13,000 ft, 3,950 m.

After an early start the next day, seven days after leaving Pokhara, Base Camp was reached by late morning and fully established by the end of the following day. The porters were paid off. On the 5 November we made our first foray into the surrounding mountains leaving Jill alone in camp with the cook. Jill's leg was hurting and she was resting when armed Khampas arrived at the camp. They looked a fearsome lot, in their traditional Tibetan red clothing with rifles and loaded bandoliers across their chests, that is, except their leader who wore western anorak and trousers. Fortunately, he could speak English.

We had heard about the Khampas, the most warlike of all Tibetans. They had a fearful reputation, known as bandits by the Chinese because of their resistance to Chinese influence in Tibet. It was known that groups, backed by the CIA, were operating in China from Mustang, just north of Johmsom but we did not think they were living so far South as our Base Camp. It transpired, however, they had a military camp about 1000 ft higher than Base Camp and had espied us from there. They enquired of Jill who were we and what were we doing camping in their area. Jill explained our situation, offering barley sugar sweets all round as a peace offering and stating that her husband would be returning 'home' soon!

They soon realised that we posed no threat to them, and with that, instead of leaving, settled down to have a picnic just outside the camp inviting Jill to join them. Jill duly did, 'enjoying' raw yak's meat, unwrapped from a bloody cloth, surprisingly, tinned fish and tsampa, a mixture of roasted barley flour and salty butter tea. Conversation flowed with the leader doing most of the talking; he explained, among other things, he had been to the cinema in India. He offered to take Jill on a white horse to the forbidden city of Muktinath. Jill politely declined but, to this day, she regrets not going; she reckons she could have coped with the leader alone but not with the dozen lieutenants with him! By then she had already noticed that there were yet more Khampas on guard surrounding them.

I did return 'home' but not till after the Khampas had left our camp. We only had dealings with them once more and they never bothered us again.

It is sad to relate that a few years later, Jill learned from a newspaper, that, following President Nixon's 'ping-pong' diplomacy with China, the CIA money, backing the Khampas, dried up and they were rounded up or killed. Also, Fred Barker, Jill's 'non-husband' for the journey to Pokhara, who seemingly was somehow involved with them, had left Fishtail Lodge.

The next day, Jill's leg was very much worse and she diagnosed thrombophlebitis. We had to evacuate her to a safer place. We tried to get her a horse from the Khampa Camp above us but, despite the fact they had horses, none was forthcoming and we eventually obtained one from the valley below. Unable to do more than hobble very slowly, Jill rode the horse whilst I accompanied her to the research station at Marpha where Pasang readily took her in. The doctor, with his wife, from Johmsom rode over on his horse to see Jill to confirm the diagnosis; but not until the social niceties had been observed and they had been given a meal. Having seen Jill, he wrote a beautifully prepared prescription. He prescribed the appropriate pills for thrombophlebitis (which he unfortunately did not possess) and additionally wrote 'Elevate the leg' which Jill had been doing anyway. He said the leg should be bound with crepe bandage but he did not have any; Jill wore two pairs of tight tights instead. He felt frustrated at not being able to do more. He did however give Jill some anti-inflammatory pills which helped.

On the summit of 'Mount High Life' 1972. Mustang and Tibet in the distance.

Lake Tilicho, Cathedral Peak and Mount 'High Life'.
16,100 ft, 4,900 m, 19,000 ft, 5,800 m, and 18,000 ft, 5,490 m respectively.

I remained with the expedition for the next nine days during which, despite two attempts to reach the frozen Tilicho Lake, we failed; we were forced back on each occasion by deep snow drifts. Richard Anderson, the leader, with another member, supported by the remaining four of us, established two higher camps in an attempt to climb an isolated 'hill' at 19,000ft which we named 'Cathedral Peak'; again, deep rotten snow, and additionally loose rock, forced them back. A lower neighbouring 'hill', at 18000 ft, similarly isolated, which we called 'Mount High Life' was climbed by myself with two other members. The view North from the summit towards Tibet was staggeringly beautiful and I wanted to go there.

On reflection, introduction of 'expedition time', by advancing our watches some three or four hours to make more use of night-time frozen snow, might have given us a better chance of reaching the Lake.

Research Station, Marpha.
8,850 ft, 2,700 m.

Meanwhile, Jill was slowly recovering, lying or sitting in the sun whenever possible, sheltering from the bitterly cold wind. She watched the colourful locals go by, invariably cheerful with lots of 'Namaste's. The people appeared more of Tibetan stock than Nepalese. Certainly, the track through was the main 'road' to Tibet with constant traffic of yaks or pack horses carrying salt southwards and anything else northwards. Some locals were anxious to stop and chat to improve their English. Invariably local men would come and chat to Pasang who held some sway in the area. After one heated debate in the local dialect which Jill listened to Pasang explained to her that they were discussing the school leaving age! Life goes on in the same way all over the world!

Pasang had two boys which he had adopted. Whilst they went to school each day and did homework, algebra one evening, by rush lamp, they were made to do many chores, catching rats, collecting firewood and water, saddling up and looking after Pasang's horse, and anything else that needed doing. On one occasion, Pasang was not pleased to learn they had spent time playing cards with Jill.

Pasang ran a remarkably well organised research station. He grew apples and a variety of vegetables; his cabbages, in particular, were massive, some weighing over 6kg. These large cabbages caused Pasang endless trouble, because the price for a cabbage was fixed in Kathmandu, based on the relatively small ones available there. He spent much time arguing with the locals over prices but, at the same time always encouraged the locals to grow their own. Pasang talked of introducing grapes to the area but whether or not he ever did, we don't know.

It was harvest time, so there was a lot of activity at the station. On one occasion, Jill remembers, lots of women noisily sorting out different types of bean with small children 'helping' their mothers in a way all children 'help' their mothers.

Pasang was, as I've already stated, well educated, he had many books and was worldly but he lived a very simple life in primitive conditions, no water, no other facilities, not even a deep trench latrine. He was kind and generous. Jill felt very privileged to be able to stay with the family for so long.

Return Journey to Pokhara.

On 18 November I went to stay with Jill at Pasang's. The expedition was packing up and, the next day, the prearranged pack horses arrived at base camp for the return journey; they were duly loaded and they set off for Pokhara. The first stop was at Marpha to pick up Jill and me but we were not quite ready.

I had found Jill in good spirits but still not yet able to walk out. A pony was eventually found and we set off to catch up with the others. We went down the valley floor crossing and recrossing the river. The pony did not like this and invariably, by way of encouragement, I would have to wade across the river first. Eventually, when we caught up with the others at lunchtime, Jill changed her pony for one of the pack horses. Again, the pack and Jill set off down the river. The rest of us walked along the track which went up and down along the western bank. We met up at Tatopani where, as we did every night, we camped. From there we were all on the track. Progress was much faster but the pack horse was just that and loved to be in the middle of the pack where Jill's leg was continuously 'bashed' by the other horses. This was even worse whenever we met, as we did at least once a day, a similar caravan of

On the return march to Pokhara, 1972.

Jill with the pack horses mid-stream in the deepest valley in the world, the Kali Gandaki. 1972

horses or yaks travelling the other way on the narrow mountain tracks sometimes with precipitous drops to the valley floor.

This continued for the next four days. Going down the steps from Ulleri, Jill marvelled at the sure-footedness of her horse. We eventually reached Pokhara where Jill, delighted to be out of the saddle, nevertheless 'thanked' her horse for the safe journey.

1974 March, April, May. Lamjung Himal, Nepal.

Shamshui Po, Hong Kong.
10 ft, 3 m.

'Please send £240 by return to confirm the booking of Lamjung Himal by the Army Mountaineering Association, (AMA) Hong Kong.' said the letter from the Government of Nepal. Knowing that the AMA had no representative in Hong Kong, this letter raised a few questions. Not least, why had the letter been addressed to me? Realising its significance, however, I duly sent off the £240 using personal money and started making enquiries. No one in the Army Headquarters knew anything about the letter so I consulted Dick Isherwood, a civilian climber I had met several times on the surrounding hills, he, climbing, and I, walking. He knew no answer but readily said he would join any such expedition.

A few days later, all became clear. Mike Burgess, a soldier like myself, telephoned to say he had just arrived in UK having been posted from Hong Kong and had travelled home via Kathmandu. There he had applied to the Nepalese Government to climb this previously unclimbed mountain which had just again come on the market and had used my name as one of the few 'climbing' military contacts he knew in Hong Kong. He would lead the expedition and told me of Frank Fonfe, whom he had met in Nepal and would be one of the climbers; he would also seek out in UK other soldiers who climbed and had the requisite experience. He explained that he intended to climb in traditional Himalayan fashion by establishing a number of camps up the mountain but we would not use Sherpas; we would do our own carrying.

Would I organise the expedition from Hong Kong? I readily agreed and told him of Dick Isherwood's wish to join us. He was delighted about

Dick whom he knew and we both acknowledged that, with several expeditions already under his belt, he was a very welcome addition.

All this happened late Summer 1973 with the permit valid for the 1974 pre-monsoon period, late-March to May. I set about arranging matters. Fundamentally, I sought authority for the expedition to be undertaken as a military exercise which would allow soldiers, military equipment, insurance, limited funds, accommodation and flights to become available. I also sought the support of Commander British Forces, General Sir Edwin Bramall; he kindly agreed to be our Patron. I also needed to make myself available; I had an understanding boss, John Edwards, and an excellent second-in-command, Mike Davidson, who was more than willing to run my squadron for me in my absence. I arranged for the gathering and storage of all expedition materiel, including that from UK, and its eventual despatch to and from Nepal.

I acted as Treasurer throughout the expedition, accounting for nearly £4,000 of cash available to me. That amount in no way, of course, reflects the true cost of what turned out to be an eleven-week expedition. On one occasion Jill walked into The Hong Kong and Shanghai Bank in Kowloon to pay-in several hundred pounds of expedition cash; she was immediately followed by a gang armed with meat cleavers, a favourite weapon locally, and firing a pistol into the ceiling. They set about robbing the bank. Jill, the only foreigner there, felt extremely vulnerable but they left her alone. The gang, having robbed the bank, fled. Jill tried to pay in her money but the shocked staff were in no state to take it and the bank was immediately closed. Still with the cash, she drove home in our open red sports car feeling even more vulnerable and felt she was being followed. Fortunately, she was not.

Dick, for his part, did sterling work in raising sponsorship from many individuals and over twenty major firms in Hong Kong including Air India who provided return tickets for all members from Hongkong to Kathmandu. He designed some ice stakes and large pitons which were made in my squadron workshop.

In the meantime in UK, Mike, in his search for climbers, found John Scott, fresh from Sandhurst, and, at the last minute, Phil Neame, still in transfer from the RAF Regiment to the Parachute Regiment. Also, in Nepal, Frank arranged for two other Gurkha soldiers to join us, Angphurba Sherpa and Sange Tamang. I, too, managed to find Derek Chamberlain, who was in the Sapper parachute squadron I had been with years before; the Squadron was visiting Hong Kong. We were now complete with climbers, all experienced in snow and ice climbing. However, given the remoteness of the area we were going to, it would be good to have a doctor accompany us. This was duly arranged with the military hospital in Hong Kong. Unfortunately, however, just before we were due to depart for Nepal, the individual concerned was posted at short notice. By default, I therefore became the 'lay doctor'; I managed a half day's 'tuition' at the hospital with the doctor and was initiated into the world of high-altitude medicine. We obtained all our medical supplies, including medicines and Mimms from the hospital. We obtained oxygen cylinders and equipment from UK for use in an emergency.

Mike, who had joined us in Hong Kong only days before, and I left there on 9 March 1974, and flew, courtesy of Air India, to Kathmandu, On the day of departure, my Chinese staff in the squadron presented me with the Hong Kong flag to fly from the summit. The expedition had started!

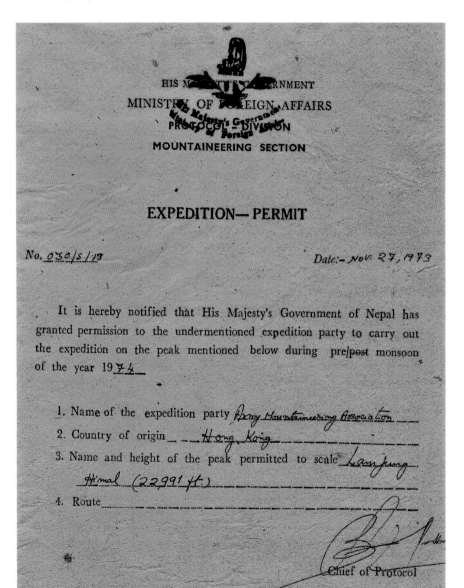

The permit for the mountain.

Kathmandu.
About 4,500 ft, 1,372 m.

The same lengthy procedures to clear customs and obtain trekking permits as we had experienced two years earlier ensued in Kathmandu. I thought I was getting to know the ropes by now but had made one big mistake. Despite it being a public holiday and the Ministry officially closed, I nevertheless had an appointment with a senior Customs official to clear our stores through customs. This was a good sign but, on our meeting, he soon realised we were not part of the major expedition to another mountain which was also in town. I believe he was just about to approve release of our equipment when he decided to examine it more closely. He spied that we were importing beef products as part of our expedition food. My heart sank, this was a real error on my part and he advised that we should resubmit our application with the offending items removed. He did add helpfully that, if we meant buffalo products, we should state as such. The forms were duly resubmitted after the holiday and approved; thereafter we all ate buffalo!

We were required to take a Nepalese Liaison Officer with us. He turned out to be a very amenable fellow but was a Kathmandu man, a Newar, not a hillman, and hated the mountains and the cold. We had to pay him and provide clothing; fortunately, the size 8 boots purchased for him by Mike in UK, in anticipation of this, fitted perfectly.

Air Reconnaissance of Lamjung.
About 23,500 ft, 7,160 m.

It had generally been accepted that the mountain would be tackled from the South via the East Col, the route taken in 1967 by a German team, albeit that attempt failed. However, that route was still subject to a detailed foot reconnaissance prior to any approach march. There was a known easy but much longer route to the foot of the mountain via the Marsyandi Khola to the North.

Hence, when the opportunity came of a relatively cheap offer to make an air reconnaissance of the mountain, we took it. Emil Wick, an experienced mountain pilot, whom Frank Fonfe knew, flew the plane, a Pilatus Porter. Making an early morning start and a full plane load, seven members of the expedition had unrivalled close-up views of both sides of the mountain. The Southern route, via the East Col, did seem to offer the best chance of success, the norther side appearing precipitous. A route beyond the East Col was identified but, whilst possible, there was no doubt that it would, in parts, be technically difficult. I knew then that beyond the East Col would be beyond my competence and I, at least, would not be reaching the top.

Emil provided further excitement that morning with a very steep descent and a late levelling off before landing at Kathmandu.

Pokhara.
About 3,000 ft, 915 m.

As before on the Tilicho expedition, we used the Pension Paying Post at Pokhara as a sorting-out base. Again, there was sufficient accommodation for us all and plenty of space to prepare for our approach march. We checked all our climbing gear, our food, fuel, tents and other equipment. It was all prioritized and numbered into basket loads as before, each typically weighing 25 to 30 kgs A Head Porter, a cook and 67 porters were hired and paid for the first few days. No clothing was given out at that stage but taken with us.

At Pokhara, armed with my new found knowledge, notes from our doctor and Mimms, I packaged the medical stores into individual kits, lead climber kits, a kit for each climbing camp and the base camp package. I briefed the other members on altitude sickness, use of the kits and instituted a buddy system for looking after each other.

Frank arranged to buy high altitude rations from another expedition which had unfortunately returned early from Daulghiri IV, following the accidental death of one of its members. These rations went a long way to providing food for the actual climb. The remaining food either had been purchased in Hong Kong or was obtained locally.

Whilst these arrangements were being made Mike and Dick reconnoitred the route; they would meet us at Jangekot, our proposed first stop.

Frank and I paying the Porters.

In charge of the buffalo.

March 23. To Jangekot.
6,500 ft, 1,980 m.

We set off from Pokhara in good order with No 1 load leading and so on but, by the time I was half way through the village, most of the porters with our loads had disappeared; home, I suppose for a meal and a last farewell but, at the time, I was a bit worried. Would we ever see them again? Fortunately, we did! By late morning we appeared complete (but not in order!).

We passed through several small villages accompanied to the end of each village by playful local children, except for two youngsters who would not leave the buffalo they were looking after. We reached Jangekot, after about 8 miles and climbing some 3,500 ft. The Porters disappeared to friends or relatives in the village, whilst the team stayed with Major Rasht Gurung, a distinguished retired Gurkha Major who was the village elder. That evening we were all entertained with Nepalese dancing, accompanied by round after round of raksi (rice whisky). Finally, we took to the floor ourselves and then we were all blessed in a traditional ceremony and wished good fortune for our climb.

March 24. To Forest Camp.
About 8,000 ft, 2450 m.

Apart from the hangovers after the jollities of the night before, it was a good start to the day on a bright sunny morning; the day did not end as well.

Before we left Jangekot I visited the local school, all the children lined up outside the school for a cleanliness and nit inspection. The children all looked remarkably clean and smart to me. The school itself was sparse in the extreme, a stone building with window openings but, of course, no glass. There were few facilities inside. There was a blackboard on the wall but no chalk. I gave the school a packet of our chalk; the thanks received were overwhelming.

On the way out of the village, some of us stopped at the village waterpoint to fill water bottles; the pump area was crowded with women in colourful clothing, chatting and laughing, some doing their clothes washing. Eventually off, we climbed steadily through the forest for about 3 hours, then into a meadow to learn that we were not on the right trail. Porters demanded a halt and were reluctant to start again that day. However, despite a severe hailstorm, which caused further delay, they were eventually persuaded to carry on. Later, with night falling, we camped on the right track but not where originally intended. We were at a site with little water which meant no cooked breakfast the next day.

Jangekot School - early morning inspection.

March 24 & 25. To Meadow with Stone Shelter.
About 9000 ft, 2,750 m.

During this day it snowed heavily resulting in two feet of snow and making progress slow. The only good thing was the beauty of the red-flowering rhododendron bushes bedecked with snow and, every now and then, fallen red petals on the snowy track. Much coaxing of porters was necessary and eventually we turned off into another meadow, this time with two stone shelters. The porters occupied the shelters whilst we camped for the night.

The next day, with more snow overnight, there was a walk-out of 47 of our porters; they were complaining about the snow and having to walk barefoot. Dick's remonstrations were of little help but some calm was established by our liaison officer, Frank and Angphurba who all, of course, spoke the local language. To each of the remaining porters, twenty of them, were issued the plimsolls, sweaters and ponchos or blankets purchased by me at Stinky's market in Hong Kong in anticipation of such a strike.

The day was getting on and it snowed again; we decided to stay where we were for the night. Given the good conditions Mike and Dick had experienced on their recce, base camp was still a good three days' march away. It was reckoned that, with the snow and number of porters left, we could reach there in six days with two carries for each leg, if everyone carried full loads. Loads were reorganised and prioritised.

The walk-out of porters.

A steep gully on the way to the Boulder Caves.

March 27 and 28. To Boulder Caves.
About 12,000 ft, 3650 m.

With a much smaller party, we left the shepherd's hut and set off, everyone carrying full loads. The porters were smiling broadly, with their new plimsols tied to their loads to keep them clean, so that some could eventually sell them. They were still barefooted, but content. The soles on their feet were generally about ten millimetres thick and they were quite happy to walk in the snow. Later, unfortunately, one porter did need regular dressings on his foot when the sole cracked in two leaving an ugly deep wound.

Over the next two days it snowed on and off and we ferried our entire stores and equipment to a spot at around 12,000 feet near some large boulders which could provide shelter for the porters. By the end of the second day, I was still feeling remarkably strong so that, when I arrived at the boulders before dispensing with my load, I did ten press-ups. By the time we later sat round our camp fire, I was beginning to feel less strong and I turned-in early. I woke in the middle of the night and had difficulty breathing. I began frothing at the mouth and, recognising the beginning of pulmonary oedema, I was just able to find and take a dose of Lasix. Still unable to breathe properly, I felt as though I was suffocating. The night dragged on and on. I kept waking up John who shared the same two-man tent. I wanted him to talk to me to stop me from falling asleep because, had I done so, I felt I would die in my sleep. At last the first signs of day break came and, between us, we got my kit packed and I was ready to start a descent. Unfortunately, Sange was also feeling unwell and had a bad dose of diarrhoea; I sat while I waited for his kit to be packed and then we both set off together with the intent of returning to Pokhara as quickly as we could possibly go. We made it in three days which, under the circumstances, was not bad going,

By the end of the first day I was feeling very much better but decided to continue on to Pokhara with Sange who was still feeling unwell. It transpired later he had amoebic dysentery and, sadly, took no further part in the expedition.

On reflection at Pokhara I realised that I had exhibited, with my press-ups, one of the early classic signs of altitude sickness, irrational behaviour; the other members of the party had failed to recognise this!

March 29 to April 7. To Pre-Base Camp.
About 13,000 ft, 3950 m.

This period covers from the time I left for Pokhara with Sange until I re-joined the main body; the record is taken, with minor amendment, from our official report[3] after the expedition.

'From the boulder-cave camp we continued, now with only fifteen porters, up steep slopes and over one section difficult enough to need a rope. Midway through the day the sun came out and, after a while, promptly brought new problems – snow blindness. The porters retired rapidly, abandoning their loads. Back at the boulder camp, we rounded up all our spare sunglasses and goggles while Angphurba, our assistant 'lay doctor', treated the sufferers. The following day, with only nine fit porters and problems compounded by the abandoned loads, we continued and managed to reach a good campsite within a day's carry of Base Camp. For the first time for nearly a week, we saw Lamjung Himal.

Three day's more carrying, with ever-more dwindling number of porters, saw us established at this campsite. The weather was now distinctly better, the snow was thawing and, especially in the morning, we had a splendid view of our mountain. At this point, however most of our porters quit. They had worked hard in the last few days on ground

---

[3]The 'Report on the Lamjung Expedition 1974' produced by Dick Isherwood and other Members of the Expedition including myself.

not without hazard and we could hardly blame them. We were left with our head porter cum cook, our mail runner and two others to assist us in carrying the last section of the route to base camp. When we counted our loads there were still sixty left. Inessentials had been left behind; it is a measure of our problems that the whisky very nearly failed to make it to base camp,'

Five further days of carrying were undertaken before I re-joined the main body at this pre-base camp on 7 April. I had spent two nights at Pokhara before returning on my own, spending two nights at Jangekot and camping for the remainder. When I arrived I learned that an advance party of Dick and Phil were already at Base camp and had made their first carry to an Advance Base on 6 April.

Phil in the avalanche area on the last leg of
the Approach March before reaching Base Camp.

The climbers near Base Camp.
Left to right: Phil, Derek, Dick, John, Mike and Frank

April 10. Lamjung Base Camp.
About 13,500 ft, 4,100 m.

After the two previous days of ferrying more stores to Base Camp, 10 April saw the 'pre-base campsite' packed up and the final carry take place. On that final day, by the time the site was cleared, it was almost mid-day when we set off. Our party was eight strong including the liaison officer; the other members of the expedition, five climbers, were already at base camp or beyond. During that march it snowed heavily for a while making our track ahead difficult to follow. Progress slowed in the deep snow and, soon afterwards, the afternoon mist rose from the valley making it even more difficult. We pressed on and, just as I was beginning to doubt we were on the right track, through the mist appeared the welcome sight of John who led us for the last mile to Base Camp. Mike had been worried about our lateness and John had volunteered to come and find us.

At last, the whole party, with the exception of Sange Tamang, and all essential stores and equipment were complete at Base camp. What had been planned to be a trek across snow-free terrain accompanied by nearly seventy porters for 5 days did not materialise. The approach march was often in deep snow, being roped up on one occasion, with over two thirds of the porters deserting us when not quite halfway and with further desertions. This necessitated expedition members having to ferry the abandoned loads in addition to their own gear to Base Camp for 14 of the 19 days it took. In that time, we had lost one climber and I had suffered a bout of altitude sickness. At least this experience had acclimatised everyone and all were looking forward to the climb itself.

I spent most of my time organising base camp. Expedition time, three hours ahead of Nepalese time, was implemented. We all found it 'easier' to get up at 6 a.m. expedition time, rather than 3 a.m. Nepalese time, in order to make best use of the early morning, cloud free, hard crisp snow. By mid-day Nepalese time, the snow had softened making walking more difficult and the clouds from the valleys below were beginning to rise soon restricting visibility. I arranged for stores to be shipped up the mountain, often carrying loads myself, accompanying others, to Advance Base at the head of a glacier and, on one occasion, to the East Col. I did not get involved in determining who would climb the mountain or at what point; that was left to Mike to agree with the other climbers.

I kept in contact with the climbers once a day by radio when conditions allowed, line of sight being the best. Keeping in contact with the outside world was almost impossible but I sent several written short reports back on progress via our mail runner. The mail generally took him two long days to reach Pokhara whence it could be delivered by road to Elizabeth Hawley in Kathmandu who handled all our mail, as she did for many expeditions; Elizabeth would then post it, including my letters to Jill in Hong Kong.

On one occasion I returned to Pokhara with the Liaison Officer to report the apparent loss of a porter, believed to have been lost in an avalanche, and to make arrangements for the recruitment of porters for the return journey. No sooner had we reached Pokhara than we saw the porter concerned who, as he smilingly explained, had had enough and decided to leave us without informing us. I did not smile! We made the due arrangements regarding porters and returned to Base Camp in a matter of days.

At Base Camp, the Liaison Officer took no interest in the mountain but had proved occasionally useful with our porters on the approach march. He remained at the camp throughout apart from the one return trip to Pokhara with me.

Two miles South of Lamjung Base Camp.
About 13,600 ft, 4,150 m.

Once, after a particularly heavy snowfall, I accompanied our runner for the first part of his journey which normally was prone to avalanche. I insisted we drop down the hillside, hopefully out of reach of any avalanche and, once past the area, we regained the normal path. The runner then went on alone and I thought I would climb up a little higher. On my own, I was just reflecting that I was very likely in an area no man had yet set foot. With that, round the mountain came a yak, its long skirt apparently hovering over the snow, accompanied by a young Tibetan girl in her everyday traditional dress. We were both surprised but she quickly recovered and bowed low with a traditional Namaste greeting, I similarly returned the greeting and, lost for words, offered her a barley sugar sweet; she most graciously accepted the sweet with cupped hands, more low bows and a beaming smile. She continued on her way, leaving only happy memories, to this day, of a magical encounter.

At that point nearing midday, when the clouds started to roll in from the valleys below, I turned back. I retraced my still visible tracks through the snow and dropped down below the avalanche area to return. Halfway across, still in the mist, there was a rumble which turned into a growing roar. I was terrified that the avalanche would reach me; then there was a deathly silence. Just after that the mist temporarily cleared revealing the end of the avalanche some two hundred metres away. I raced on to the safety of Base Camp.

Left to Right: The Runner, Angphurba Sherpa, Liaison Officer with me preparing a note for the Runner. Lamjung forms the backdrop

April 10. Advance Base.
15,500 ft, 4,725 m.

This camp was situated in a snow bowl at the head of a glacier on a fairly level plateau, the crossing of which was generally undertaken roped up because of several crevasses. The plateau was reached via an icefall which itself was about a mile from Base Camp. Dick and Phil made the first carry to this site in deep powder snow, taking five and a half hours on 6 April. Over the next few days more carries established the camp on 10 April when Dick and Phil slept there. Eventually, with an early start and good conditions, the carry time from Base to Advance Base was reduced to two hours.

April 15. Camp I.
17,800ft, 5,427m.

Camp 1 is on the East Col attained via a snow ramp which reaches the ridge at 5488 m (18,000 ft), the highest point reached by me on this expedition. The first carry to the camp by Dick and Phil took place on 11 April; daily carries by them both plus Frank followed and the camp was occupied on 15 April. On one of these climbs Frank fell and slid a long way down the ramp; remarkably, only his pride was hurt but the contents of his pack, mainly food, were scattered everywhere.

April 16. Snowhole, Lamjung.
About 18,900 ft, 5750 m.

Phil and Dick made an initial carry up the slopes above the East Col, taking a line of snow couloirs and ridges on the northern flank of the East ridge so as to avoid the lower, rocky part of the ridge. The views here were magnificent, over the mountains North of the Marsyandi Khola and

Dropping down from the top of the snow ramp to Camp 1 on the East Col.

At the top of the snow ramp above the East Col.

91

the great trio of Manaslu, Peak 29 and Himalchuli rising to the East beyond the Lamjung Pinnacle also lying to the East of the col. They found the ridge, when reached, to be rather narrow, fragile and capped in sugary snow; their progress along it was fairly slow. In parts it seemed best to break down the whole crest until it was wide and solid enough on which to walk. After some five hours they reached a small crest from which point conditions on the ridge deteriorated further. From there a thousand feet of very narrow, steep sided corniced ridge led to the serac wall which they had identified from below as one of their major obstacles. It then appeared that this ridge rather than the seracs themselves would be the crux of the climb. It was clear that fixed ropes were needed on this section to allow the higher camps to be stocked. A further problem was that there was no site on the ridge wide enough to pitch a tent. Phil and Dick found the next best thing, a site for an ice cave, albeit in a hair-raising position. They then made a start on digging the cave but, as it was getting late, put what stores they could in it, left the remainder alongside and returned to Camp 1.

It was then realised that all the equipment for fixed ropes was still at base camp. I arranged for the equipment to be carried up. I was delighted that the three-foot snow belay stakes and large pitons, those made by my squadron and the subject of many jokes about their size and weight, were now required; they were to prove invaluable.

April 19 and 20. Camp 2.
19,800 ft, 6036 m.

Mike and John moved to the front and went to the embryo ice cave, supported by Phil, Dick and Derek. Mike's and John's tasks were to fix ropes along or around the ridge, find a way up the serac wall and site Camp 2. They dropped down some 100 feet below the ridge on the North side, traversed the slope and climbed back up to the ridge at the foot of the seracs, fixing a total of eight ropes over difficult ground on unstable snow. It was in this section the oversized stakes proved their worth; they were difficult to install but, once in, never moved. They slept one night in the ice cave which John had enlarged to accommodate them as well as all the stores. They had a reasonable night in the cave, drips from the roof being the only problem.

On the second day they found a way though the seracs, fixed two ropes and found a site for Camp 2, albeit in a crevasse on the edge of a very large drop. Sheltered as it appeared to be, powder snow, blown from the upper slopes of the mountain, nevertheless accumulated around the tents. On the third morning, 21 April, firing a red Verey light, a prearranged signal, called Phil, Dick and Derek to join them. The three carried only one tent between them in order to save weight. A very crowded night in the 2-man tent ensued but it was hoped, and it later transpired, they had done the last carry up the mountain without the need for further resupply.

Unfortunately, at this stage Mike contracted a heavy cold and was forced to retreat to Camp 1 to rest. At least, this had the advantage of levelling the tent situation. An initial attempt on the summit was made by Phil and Derek with Dick and John following on a day behind. Each party was essentially self-contained carrying a tent, food, cooking and climbing gear. They went up light with around 40 lb each, while John and Dick, aiming to support them, carried extra fuel and food and had initially around 60 lb apiece.

Reaching the top of the Lamjung East ridge above the East Col.

Fixing a rope on the North slope.

April 23 and 24. Camp 3.
21,500 ft, 6555 m.

The route above the crevasse camp lay across a narrow and fragile ice bridge, then up steepish ice and snow for 300ft to the main East ridge which, as we had all seen from our aerial reconnaissance, led without much difficulty to the summit area. Route finding difficulties and poor weather caused Phil and Derek to camp early on their first day at around 20,500 ft. There, in an exposed campsite, they were within sight of Base Camp, 7000 ft below, but they were not seen from there as cloud surrounded the upper slopes of Lamjung for most of the day.

On their second day, Phil and Derek continued over mainly straightforward ground to another windy campsite just above the snow dome which forms a conspicuous landmark on the ridge. The highlight of this day's climb was a short overhanging ice climb which necessitated the use of ice pitons. Climbing the overhang and hauling their 40lb sacks at 21,000 ft was a fairly strenuous business they discovered.

Mike on the fixed rope on the North side of the East ridge.

Camp 2.

Derek on the Summit flying the Hong Kong Flag.

Derek on the last pitch.

April 25 to May 3. Summit of Lamjung.
22,911 ft, 6983 m.

At 6am Nepalese time, Phil and Derek set out for the summit in a viciously cold wind which slowed their progress considerably; in all they had about another 1,500 ft to climb. The first 1000 ft was straight-forward snow but the final section presented, at this altitude, several time-consuming problems. Three rope lengths of steep and fairly difficult ice led to a knife-edged corniced snow ridge and a forty-foot wall of near vertical snow ice. At 3.30 pm they reached the summit, a long undulating snow ridge. The Hong Kong and Nepalese flags were duly flown. For a time, they were fortunate to have a clearing in the weather in which to take photographs and admire the view, West to the bulk of Annapurna 2 and East to the Manaslu range. After a careful descent of the difficult wall and ridge section they returned to Camp 3 just before dark.

John and Dick made the second ascent of Lamjung by the same route, passing the first ascent party on their way down; they reached the summit on the 27 April. They were less fortunate with the weather and had to retreat from the summit with an electric storm buzzing around their heads. Descending the summit wall they had a fright when an abseil piton, which had supported Dick, pulled out under John's greater weight just as he was reaching the foot of the wall. They continued their descent with circumspection. Two days later they reached Camp 1 and had a prolonged rest.

John on the last pitch.

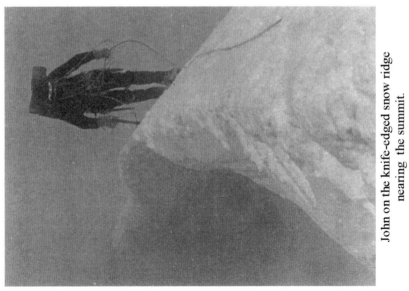

John on the knife-edged snow ridge nearing the summit.

John and Dick, on their return, found that Mike was recovering well and making plans to climb to the top as well. Although Frank had come up to Camp 1, he had already decided, after his long fall, that was as far as he was going. Following a dream he had of his uncle, who had died on Everest, beckoning him up the mountain, Angphurba too had decided he was not going beyond Camp 1. Mike therefore at first considered a solo trip but Phil, who had by that time rested, volunteered to go up with him. He and Mike set out from Camp 1 on 30 April following the same route and using the two tents left by the two previous pairs. They were delayed by sickness and fatigue but were able to leave Camp 3 for the summit on 3 May. Below the final summit wall the effects of Phil's previous exertions showed again and he stopped there. Mike climbed the final section alone and was rewarded with better visibility than either of the other parties. He and Phil descended uneventfully and were back at Camp 1 on 5 May.

Base Camp Packed and return to Pokhara and on to Kathmandu.

After much heart-searching it was decided to leave the fixed ropes between Camps 1 and 2 as removing them would have been a prolonged operation and, for a fatigued party, a risky one. Camp 1 was packed and, en route, Advanced Base; these were carried down to Base Camp on 7 May. Base camp was packed and the main body set off for Pokhara on 9 May, complete with sufficient porters to carry everything. Pokhara was reached on 12 May and Kathmandhu a few days later. The Embassy kindly laid on a party for us.

Arrival in Hong Kong and Reflections.

We were exceedingly lucky to return without serious injury. Frank's long fall on the way to Camp 1 and John's short fall on the overhang near the summit could have turned out very differently, with recovery, if possible at all, extremely difficult and time consuming. All suffered, to varying degrees, the effects of altitude, sore throats, headaches, rasping coughs and lack of sleep. Mike did particularly well not to succumb to his cold and sat it out, on his own, at Camp 1. I can confirm that, with serious altitude sickness, the only solution is to descend the mountain as quickly as possible. Not surprisingly, we all lost weight; I lost over two stones.

On arrival back in Hong Kong, much was made for a while in the local press of our success.

I, not really a climber, felt very privileged to be part of the team. I take my hat off to the other members who all contributed significantly to the success of the expedition; in particular, reaching base camp in the first instance, despite the loss of our porters, and carrying loads up the mountain. In particular I heartily congratulate the five climbers who overcame a number of technical difficulties at altitude to reach the summit; all showed great spirit and determination.

Dick Isherwood went on to become a well-known climber in Alpine circles and undertook several expeditions in China and elsewhere. John Scott and Phil Neame later joined the Joint Services Expedition to climb Everest, both declaring that Everest, apart from the problems posed by the increased height, was technically easier than Lamjung. John, in typical fashion, near the top turned back to accompany an ailing person back down the mountain. He continued climbing throughout his life and became a lead member of a Mountain Rescue Team in the Lake District. Phil, who, having already been to the top of Lamjung very generously accompanied Mike on his bid, organised another expedition to Everest. Whilst not summitting, he turned the experience into the foundation stone for a charity, The Ulysses Trust, to fund TA soldiers on adventurous training. Derek, the youngest of us, then aged 20, was recorded at the time as the youngest person to have made a first ascent of such a height. It always made us laugh that, ironically, his home was in Spalding, a low flat area of England.

Unfortunately, Dick and John have both since died along with Mike, who died in a climbing accident, and Frank, in a parachuting accident. With the other members in Nepal, and Phil temporarily ill, that left Derek, his wife, myself with Jill and family to meet in 2014 at Seatoller House and celebrate, forty years on, the success of the expedition. Tabitha made a cake for the occasion and Derek and I gave a short informal talk about the expedition to the other guests staying there. We shall see whether we meet in 2024!

Tabitha's Lamjung Cake.

1987. Nepal to Pakistan via Tibet Autonomous Region and China.

Kathmandu.
About 4,500 ft, 1,372 m.

Again, Kathmandu provided the starting point for this trip into Tibet, into China and eventually westwards into Pakistan, a distance of some 1500 miles. Jill and I proposed to travel to China as independent travellers, and, as such, did not need a guide as we would if we were part of a group. Nevertheless, we set off with seven other people, all similarly independent travellers intent on the same trip.

We set off together in good order in a hired minibus which took us out eastwards for a couple of hours before we were halted by a landslide. We walked across the slide and, thereafter, each of us caught whatever transport we could between other landslides and so made our way to the Friendship Bridge, across the Sun Kosi River, which marked the border with Tibet.

Mountain Passes on Tibetan Plateau.
About 16,000 ft, 4,900 m.

After our first night in Tibet, at Zhangmu, Jill and I were up first, our fellow travellers still abed. The door of the Hotel was locked so we could not get out; eventually we found the caretaker asleep under the counter. He very reluctantly opened the door and was about to lock up again; we did a charade trying to explain that others would also soon be leaving. He looked puzzled, we left.

We walked to the café we had been to the night before; it had not impressed us then but, as it was the only café, we had little option but to give it another chance. It was still dark and the café, a wooden shed, was padlocked from the outside. We banged on the window and, surprisingly, a key was passed to us through a crack in the door. I unlocked the padlock and let ourselves in; the owner was just about to light a fire to cook breakfast. It was very cold outside and as there was no sign of anyone else, we waited for breakfast. One and a half hours later we were served slushy rice and pieces of dough boiled in a dreadful tasting brown liquid. By then we had been joined by another traveller who reckoned the market was wide open for Kellogs!

Soon after, our porters, who were to carry our gear up to our transport at the top of the hill, also arrived; they collected our gear and set off quickly ahead of us. We too, more slowly, set off and found ourselves in the middle of a funeral procession. Apparently, a woman had been murdered for her necklace and was now on her way to a sky burial, with mournful music from conch cells and huge horns, her body wrapped in a sheet and slung from two poles.

When we reached our transport, the bus had a flat tyre. We waited whilst the puncture was repaired and tyre reinflated with a hand pump. During this time we all became the centre of attraction, midst a gathering of inquisitive Tibetans who wanted to take, and did take, many photographs with our cameras.

At last we set off, travelling through fantastic scenery, sheer cliffs, huge waterfalls and the road winding and rising in a series of hairpin bends, often with precipitous drops to the river below. There was hardly any vegetation on the high plateau; exceptionally, there were small areas which had been cultivated and the crops were being harvested with the aid of yaks. The villagers, all in traditional costume, were as cheerful and colourful as ever.

We climbed over three passes and at each the area was a colourful mass of fluttering prayer flags. These areas were generally prone to high winds and the flags, as they sent their prayers skywards, made a continuous humming noise. From one of these high points, not too far from the entrance to the Rongbuk valley, the route taken by the early Everest mountaineers, we had a magnificent view of Everest. Its white plume, extending downwind from the summit, clearly visible against the blue sky.

By the time we arrived at the last pass at about 16,500 ft, 5000 m most of us were feeling nauseous and had headaches, the altitude taking its toll. At 10 p.m. we arrived at our overnight stop at Lhatse; it had been a very long and tiring day. We stayed in a very basic bus halt. Four iron bedsteads to a small room off the bus yard; no light, no water, no facilities! We nevertheless slept reasonably well!

Lhasa, Tibet.
About 12,000 ft, 3,650 m.

We arrived in Lhasa after two further days travelling, via Shigatse and Gyantse. The Tashi Lhunpo monastery at Shigatse is the traditional home of the Panchen Lama, second in the Buddhist hierarchy after the Dalai Lama. Following the Chinese takeover, the exact whereabouts of the Panchen Lama seemed to be not known.

The day before we arrived in Lahsa, the monks, protesting at the increasing Chinese influence in the country, had burnt down the police station; the station was still smouldering. So was the atmosphere in the city, there was a tenseness in the air which was palpable.

Nevertheless, daily life continued. Barkhor Square was colourfully crowded, including many pilgrims, with some continuing, as they had done so since the start of their pilgrimage, to measure their length as they made their way into the sacred Jokang Temple. Jill and I entered through a side door to find long walls of huge prayer wheels and rows of butter lamps flickering in the otherwise dark shadows. There were many pilgrims inside the temple court yard and whole families were sitting in the sun; some shrines contained wonderful old brass and copper pots as well as brightly coloured Buddhas and wall hangings.

Typical array of prayer flags at Himalayan mountain passes in Tibet.

Pilgrims 'measuring their length', Barkhor Square Temple, Lhasa. 1987.

The narrow streets immediately surrounding the Temple were also part of the pilgrimage; pilgrims gained extra merit towards enlightenment and warded off misfortune by circling the temple three times, on their 'kora'. These streets were, not surprisingly, crowded and noisy, lined as they were with small shops and stalls all bidding for trade; there were also many individual walking street vendors. These Tibetan ladies were full of fun trying to sell us delightful souvenirs and very pretty turquoise and silver rings and necklaces.

After lunch on a roof terrace overlooking the square, we made our way to the Potala Palace, the former home of the Dalai Llama. The seven storey palace formed a magnificent sight dominating the skyline. Unfortunately, we found it closed for the day. We then visited an art gallery with many colourful Tibetan paintings and a small 'village' at the foot of the Potala which was entirely Tibetan, apparently then untouched by any Chinese influence. A walk through the Potala park followed; it was a popular meeting place, having a lake with carp and an island housing the Serpent Temple. Leaving the park Jill had her sandals mended by a local cobbler.

When we woke the next morning to a bright sunny day, we noticed that snow had fallen on the surrounding hills; this backdrop seemed to add a new enhancing dimension to the brown and white Potala. We were determined to visit and were not disappointed. We walked up the zig-zag step way, the only foreigners amid a host of Tibetan pilgrims, men, women and children happily either chatting or chanting. Some women had their hair braided in the traditional 108 small braids, all tied and linked around their shoulders. We bought tickets and entered a central courtyard where there were the toilets, the locations of which we always took note. In this case they were lovely wooden slit loos along the outer walls of the Potala with very long drops beneath.

We had heard that the Potala had been ransacked by the Chinese but it had not; the Palace appeared untouched. The Dalai Lama's room 'remained untouched and was as he had left it' Elsewhere there were lots of paintings, shrines, wall hangings, murals, butter lamps, butter carvings and incense burners. The Tibetan pilgrims were leaving their own offerings, often adding butter to the lamps, leaving handfuls of grain at the shrines, spinning the prayer wheels and ringing bells. The huge gold and bejewelled tombs of former Dalai Lamas were there, the gold 'as thick as yak hide'.

Delighted with our morning's visit, we hired a couple of bicycles and set off to the Drephung Monastery just out of town. Again, we were the only foreigners there. Hardly were we inside, when we were advised to leave by the monks. After a very rapid tour of the monastery, we did leave and had biked away no further than a couple of hundred yards when we were held at gunpoint by Chinese soldiers.

We were told to get off our bikes and wait. We looked around to see soldiers in all the surrounding fields moving in on the monastery. Eventually a jeep-type vehicle arrived and out got a leather-bomber-jacketed person in civilian clothes and dark sunglasses who immediately asked us what we were doing in the monastery. Who were we? Why did we visit? 'Do you know to whom you are speaking?' thought I, without mouthing it, and also thought this is not the time to take that line! Quiet, polite answers seemed to do the trick and he suddenly told the soldiers to lower their guns and let us go. We sped off and sadly to this day, I am ashamed to say, we never did know the fate of that monastery.

We hurriedly left Lhasa the next day by bus and headed further into China; from the bus we saw a seemingly endless convoy of army vehicles all carrying armed soldiers driving into Lhasa.

Butter Lamps in Jokhang Temple, Lhasa.

A couple of wealthy Tibetans, Lhasa.

The Potala Palace, Lhasa.

Cobbler mending Jill's sandals, Lhasa 1987.

Golmud, China.
9,216 ft, 2,810 m.

Leaving Lhasa, we travelled for several days in a series of local buses. We either passed through or stayed overnight in the odd village. One large town, in particular, is worthy of mention, Golmud. Now, this is a place I would strongly recommend that you avoid at all costs. Covered in a yellowy smog, which forced all the locals to wear face masks, it appeared as no more than one huge chemical works, set in a desert.

Trying to escape back to that desert for a breath of fresh air and a picnic, we hired a couple of bikes but were turned back by armed Chinese soldiers on the main road out of the city. We backed off, rounded a corner out of sight of the guards, went a few hundred yards down a small dirt track into the start of the desert and did have our picnic - in a large drainage ditch out of sight of everyone.

The town did, however, provide some fun. We went into a supermarket; a huge emporium with virtually empty shelves, but lots of shop assistants. The only things for sale, as far as we could tell, were a motorbike, tins of mandarin oranges and packs of cards. In our faltering finger-pointing sign language we made it known we wanted a tin of oranges and a pack of cards; we were quickly served and soon on our way.

We returned to our digs for a game of cards, shuffled the pack and started playing. It was not too long before we noticed the lack of spades and plenty of clubs; in fact, two sets of clubs. We returned to the shop where they were pleased to see us again but failed to understand our much clubbing and little digging action sign language. Even after we laid out all fifty-two cards, they failed to comprehend the idea of a returns policy for an opened pack of cards. As soon as I asked to see the head man of the shop I regretted it. What if it's the same guy in the leather jacket and dark glasses who saw us off in Lhasa? However, it was not and we get did get another pack of cards. To this day I also regret we did

Serious political riots have taken place recently in Lhasa and other places of Tibet stirred up by a few separists on the purpose to separate Tibet from China and to destroy the situation of stability and unity. In order to guarantee the safety of Tibetans who want to go on pilgrimage in Lhasa, overseas Chinese from Hongkong, Macau and Taiwan as well as the foreigners, we give the following notice.

1. According to the higher authority's instruction, neither overseas Chinese from Hongkong, Macau and Taiwan nor foreigners are permitted to enter into Tibet whether they have got entry visas or not. If anyone wants to leave China through Tibet, please change the route.

2. Owing to the poorer public order in Tibet, all temple will be closed temporarily. The Tibet masses who intend to go on pilgrimage in Lhasa are required to go back home and settle down to productive work. Pilgrimage may be gone on when the situation takes a favourable turn.

3. From now on, no vehicle either belongs to State or collective or private person is permitted to pick up Tibetan overseas to enter into Tibet. The tickets for Lhasa bought by the passengers should be taken back, the passengers can get refund for tickets.

Issued by
The Gouvernent of Golmud

October 8 1987

A Transcription of the notice.

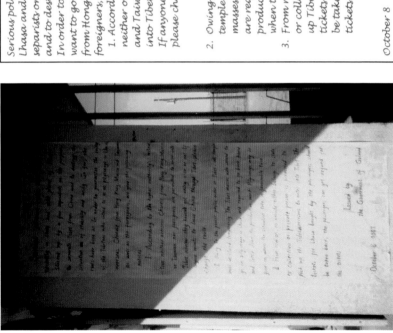

The actual handwritten notice to foreigners, posted in our hotel in Golmud.

113

not keep the first pack. We could have had so much fun with them; just imagine the bridge games we might have had!

When we returned to our hotel there was a handwritten notice in English on display by the entrance, signed by the Governor of the Province. The notice exhorted the locals to return to their homes and farm peaceably and not riot; foreigners, including Hong Kong Chinese, were not to go to Lhasa but return to their own country straightaway. We left the next morning by bus heading further into China.

Dunhuang, China.
3,734 ft, 1,138 m.

When the bus arrived in the bus station at Golmud there was a great scrum to get on it despite us having numbered seats allotted. At first Jill was squashed at the entrance steps unable to lift a foot to get on board; it was a real fight. Eventually we got our seats but some people had to stand for the twelve-hour journey to Dunhuang. It was still dark when we set off and it was cold; we drove over a very bleak landscape of salt flats passing the occasional salt mine.

We stopped for lunch in a dirty, enclosed yard where Jill went to 'the worst loo in the world'. A pit, already overflowing, with rocking logs over it on which one had to squat. Jill says she was squatting down trying not to breathe, when a Chinese woman next to her lost her balance and grabbed her nearly sending them both into the stinking pit, much to the amusement of several other women onlookers.

We continued on our way along a very dusty track; the dust came up through the bus floorboards and covered everyone. We arrived at Dunhuang in the evening and we booked into a nearby modern-looking hotel. This was exceptional in that the staff were extremely helpful and quickly gave us a cup of Chinese tea; this was most welcome as we were parched by the dust. We tried to clean our very dusty luggage, which had been on top of the bus, before taking it to our room because this hotel was by far the cleanest we had ever stayed in on this trip. We noticed it was a three bedded room and wondered who else might join us as seemed customary in such cases; fortunately, no one did. There was a decent loo at the end of the corridor and, amazingly, a hotel laundry service which was much needed. That evening we walked along the road and found a small café where we were allowed to go into the kitchen, choose the food and watch it being stir fried over a wood fire. We had rice, egg and vegetables which was excellent. Things were looking up; so far Dunhuang had done us proud!

Gleaming pans in a Tibetan café kitchen.

The Caves of a Thousand Buddhas.

Next morning, we were back on a bus by 8am, this time to visit the Caves of a Thousand Buddhas; caves, we later learned, from which early explorers had removed various artefacts which were apparently now in Britain. On arrival we first had to get tickets which itself proved a bit of a hassle; our cameras and bags were taken from us, then we could start our tour. 'Where is your guide? What no guide?' we imagined they said to us in rapid Chinese. Eventually after some time, a guide was obtained for us but she too could speak no English. This guide in any case did not have the keys to the caves. More waiting until, much later, our guide reappeared with the keys. Most of the morning had gone so we only saw a few caves, each unlocked and locked again after we left. We were disappointed in what we had seen because several of the wall paintings had been recently repainted, rather badly we thought, as part of a restoration project. Jill and I did manage, however, having said goodbye to our guide, to see inside an unlocked pagoda which contained a huge sitting Buddha; this was magnificent. We then rushed to catch a bus into Dunhuang so that we had time to explore the place as we were leaving the next day.

Dunhuang is at the crossroads of the North-South, India to Mongolia, route and the East-West Silk road. As such it is relatively cosmopolitan and a centre, among other things, for arts and crafts; we saw bright, coloured jewellery, silkworks and other artistic work including a large selection of jade carvings. At the cotton market we saw huge piles of cotton being unloaded from small donkey carts, the general 'workhorse' of the area. We bought some fruit from the fruit and vegetable market where again we saw the donkey carts arriving from the fields with their loads. We watched whilst some sort of flat doughnut was made at a street stall; with flavoured sugar inside; it tasted delicious.

In the early evening we caught another bus to the great sand dunes nearby. Like good tourists we could not resist a ride on a Bactrian camel before climbing a huge dune to watch a glorious sunset.

A donkey cart carrying cotton.

Riding on the dunes.

Dunhuang to Kashgar via Urumchi and Turfan
98 ft, 30 m.

Having bussed from Dunhuang to Lu Wan, caught an overnight train through desolate Black Gobi hills, we arrived in Urumchi. We bussed to Turfan where we spent a restful couple of days, except we had to share our room with a Chinese man also staying at the hotel. The Town is noted for being on the northern edge of a massive, below sea-level, depression as mentioned earlier; its ancient irrigation system feeds grapes growing seemingly everywhere, notably providing vine-growing trellises making shady walkways within the Town itself. The only downside was the constant loud speakers blaring out Chinese 'messages' to the indigenous locals, predominately Uighers. A bus back to Urumchi, an overnight stopover there and an 'exciting' aircraft ride along the Tian Shan mountain range saw us arrive late evening in Kashgar. A massive, 'everyman for himself' scrum to recover our luggage dumped in a small room was seemingly necessary before we eventually disgorged from the airport, somewhat dishevelled and tired. A pony and trap carried our luggage into town whilst we walked alongside.

A drying shed used to produce sultanas, near Turfan.

A noodle shop in Turfan.

Kashgar, West China.
4,170 ft, 1,271 m.

Jill and I stayed a couple of full days in Kashgar, a market town in the far West of China, the home of the Uigher people and near the border with the then USSR. For the first of the three nights, we stayed at the Seman Hotel. We had heard that hotel was a former Russian Embassy. However, my dream of grand staircases and chandeliers was short lived; the room, admittedly better than the first we were shown, was damp and, apart from two iron bedsteads, otherwise devoid of furniture. The bedsteads were bare, no bed clothes, but we had our sleeping bags. Piled bricks comprised five of the eight legs. Under both beds, there was a lot of litter and an empty beer bottle. The loo was in an adjacent room. The floor of this 'en suite', which fortunately had a step down into it, was flooded with about 4 inches of water; in this floor was a hole, the loo, just discernible in the flood. We stayed there the first night because, at least, it had a roof; we were tired and had arrived late in the evening. Despite a good night's sleep, first thing the next morning, we moved to a nearby hotel. Even this hotel had few facilities but, at least, it did not smell.

Once installed, we set off walking towards the Sunday market. All along the way were pony carts full of families, many with goods to sell. Before long, we too got a lift in a pony cart to the market, the method of transport with very few cars about. Some of the ponies have strings of beads and bells around their necks and on a loop over their heads. The whole town resounds to this jingle-jangle which starts before dawn. When we arrived at the market, we watched our driver, along with many others, unhitch his pony and put his cart, upended, in the designated cart park. All very well we thought but how on earth does he find his cart at the end of the day amidst the hundreds of other, seemingly identical, carts?

121

Pony cart traffic toing and froing near the market.

The market cart park, Kashgar 1987.

In the saddle before buying.

Bargaining.

At the market we bought a picnic breakfast and sat for a while watching the ever-bustling scene before us. There were hundreds of people about the market, some on foot, many riding horses, others pushing hand carts, all jostling for space. We went to the livestock area and watched the horses being put through their paces, ridden at speed through the crowds, teeth examined and prodded all over before the bargaining took place. Camels, sheep, goats, cows, donkeys, more ponies, chickens and ducks were also being sold. At the fruit area, we feasted on the mouth-watering melons and pomegranates along with other fruit, nuts and vegetables. Elsewhere, ironmongers, tinsmiths, blacksmiths, hatters, bootmakers, clothiers, basket makers and medicine-men were all practising their trade and selling their wares; the blacksmiths were making and mending various implements as well as shoeing horses, ponies and donkeys; tinsmiths were making and mending the tin stoves on which most of the food is cooked.

There were huge piles of timber stacked up with ready-made doors and windows available for sale; people would be carrying long lengths of timber through the crowds shouting for others to make way. We watched cobblers fix what appeared to be little horseshoes to boots; we watched barbers with cut-throats shaving men's heads; no wonder the men needed to wear their fur-clad hats. Their clothing and boots seemed to be of good quality, warm and thick; they good-naturedly spurned my relatively high-tech lightweight jacket. I tried on some of the hats to the amusement of the crowd and did buy one which, years later, provided a good home for a thousand bugs. It was all such fun for us. Jill said it was like being 'in the middle of a Thomas Hardy film'. At the end of a long but thoroughly enjoyable day we walked back through the twilight to our new hotel; the jingle-jangle still in the air. The day ended perfectly with supper by the same 'hole in the wall' cafe we had found the night before. The café sold chips, the first in China we had come across.

Mouth-watering melons.

Pomegranates.

Basket maker.

Medicine Man.

In 1987 we were privileged to witness the Uighurs as a proud people; the men, dressed in their thick leather and woollen clothing and seemingly born to ride horses. At that time, the local population was almost entirely Uigher with but few Han Chinese about. Sadly, that is no longer the case and suppression of the Uighers seems to be the norm. With the now strong Chinese influence we understand Kashgar market is much smaller, indoors and there are large quantities of cheap Chinese plastic goods for sale.

When, two years later, Tim and Sue visited Kashgar, they also visited the market which was, at that time, still an open market and much as we had seen. However, it was at Kashgar they witnessed a man being beaten up, apparently a thief. He was continually prodded with an electric cattle prod by the Chinese police and, eventually, shot and killed by them. This clearly upset Tim and Sue as well as two friends who also happened to be in Kashgar. When they all expressed some sympathy for the poor man they were not popular with some of the other onlookers. All four hurriedly left Kashgar.

On the way home from the timber market.

A close shave.

Fruit stall in town, Kashgar.

A carpet maker of Kashgar.

Engrossed in the spinning top.

Home-made toy cars, Kashgar-style, 1987.

Khunjerab Pass, China.
About 15,450 ft, 4,710 m.

Leaving Kashgar by 'international air-conditioned bus' sounds too good to be true - and it was! The bus was certainly 'international' in that it connected two countries but being 'air-conditioned' meant that the driver would not let us open the windows despite the fact that the air-conditioning did not work, and clearly had not for years, For a start, the bus was six hours late, although that might have been our problem as there was always confusion as to whether we were on local time or Beijing time. Also, when the bus did arrive, we could not leave until we had filled in six copies of customs forms; we were required to declare precisely, among other items, just how many sewing machines, and the number of washing machines, we were exporting to Pakistan.

The bus itself was battered and looked tired. It broke down twice on the journey, once in the middle of nowhere, except the whole journey seemed to be in the middle of nowhere, as we skirted the western fringes of the Taklamakan desert. Breakdowns, to be fair, caused no more than several hours delay at a time. The driver was more than competent at improvisation and carried on his bus a large stock of spares; the first time replacing a broken suspension spring. At least these stops, along with prayer times later in Pakistan, provided the opportunity, I should say the only opportunity, to go to the loo. There was an ever-present smell of diesel on board as the extra fuel cans carried obviously leaked; even our flat bread with Bovril, for me, and Marmite, for Jill, tasted of diesel.

This is not to say our journey was without fun. We were travelling with several Pakistanis who were jubilant at the prospect of returning home and they kept us entertained with their renderings of different songs. On one night stop, in a lone concrete building, but still in the middle of nowhere, we were all woken from our sleep by the bus driver who wanted to reconcile the number of passengers with the number of tickets purchased.

131

Where the bus broke down on the road to Pakistan 1987.

Bactrian Camels from the road to Pakistan.

Naturally enough, there was no electricity; it was pitch black and he came into the one room, where all of us were, with a single torch. Awoken so suddenly as we were, few could find their tickets in the dark. Fortunately, some did find theirs and, after due inspection, these were passed in the dark to those without until the driver was satisfied that everyone had shown him a ticket. Getting to sleep after that hilarious interlude took some doing. The next morning, those who slept in late did not miss the bus because the bus would not start; its engine frozen. Eventually, a blow torch applied to the sump and other parts did the trick. The next night was in a yurt on the outskirts of Tashkurgen.

The nearer we got to Pakistan the worse the road became. We often had to get out and walk alongside the bus as it crossed stretches of boulders where the road was yet to be finished. At one point we passed a party of prisoners, with their armed guards, working on the road. Eventually we made it to the pass which is firmly in Chinese hands. We stopped on top to allow the bus engine to cool down; we got out and went to the loo where the solid matter was piled high, frozen and sticking up through the hole provided.

The border was a few miles southwards across the pass. There that bus journey ended and we caught another, smaller, bus onwards. Unfortunately, our fellow Pakistani travellers could not continue with us as they were delayed at the border because of the number of sewing machines and washing machines they wanted to import. Our trip from Kashgar to the Pass had taken three days, a journey which Tim and Sue would undertake in the future in one day, along a smooth new highway.

The Khunjerab pass is at the northern end of the Karakoram Highway and at the western end of the Karakorum mountain range. The range contains several mountains over 7,000 m and four over 8,000 m, including K2 at 28,250 ft, 8611m.

In the middle of Nowhere!

Our bus on a difficult section approaching the Pass.
Prisoners mending the road.

Peshawar, Pakistan.
1,060 ft, 323 m.

We arrived in Peshawar, the Southern end of the Karakoram Highway late in the evening. We had travelled some 3,600 miles since leaving Kathmandu, three weeks earlier, approximately 720 miles by air, 360 by train and the remainder by bus. Tired by this last leg, amid the bustling crowds of the station, we obviously looked lost. 'Take them to the English Hotel.' a local said and, with that, we were bundled into a bicycle rickshaw and off we were taken. The 'English Hotel' proved a haven of peace and comfort, the neat green lawns, the hot baths and hot meals of Dean's Hotel.

Despite the several landslides which delayed us by a couple of days, we had 'rushed' down the Karakoram Highway in order to catch our plane in Peshawar, and so, according to our local fellow travellers on the bus, 'missed the best scenery in the world' We were anxious to return and do justice to the area.

The Khunjerab Pass, firmly in Chinese hands.

Dean's Hotel. Now understood to be demolished.

Walking across a typical landslide on the Karakoram Highway.
Stones continuously falling.

1989. Naltar Valley Trek, Baltistan, Pakistan.

Peshawar.
1,060 ft, 323 m.

We did return to Peshawar two years later to meet Tim and Sue who were backpacking their way around Asia. We had actually met Tim and Sue before Peshawar when we arrived in the country, at Islamabad. Intent on catching a bus from the airport into Town, we did our usual trick of not making eye contact with the local taxi touts. Jill was therefore surprised, to say the least, to see me actually embracing one of them who had been particularly insistent; it was Tim. Dressed in local costume, heavily suntanned with a black beard, he was virtually indistinguishable from the touts.

Together we visited the local area and, in the North, the Hunza valley. Sadly, this whole northern area was taken over by the Taliban and, I imagine, it is still not safe for travellers.

Regimental Crests of regiments, British and local, that have guarded the Pass.

With Tim. The Afghan border behind us.

Khyber Pass and Landi Khotal.
3,610 ft, 1,100 m.

Quite how Jill persuaded the local Tourist Minister in Peshawar to allow us to drive the length of the Pass, which was forbidden territory to foreigners, I don't know, but she did! - provided we took an armed guard from the Pakistan Army with us. This was necessary as the Pass and neighbouring area were notoriously lawless and had always been so. The Pass was guarded by the Pakistan Army which had in 1947 replaced the many British, and British officered, regiments formerly based there including that of both my grandfathers. Regimental crests remain there on the mountainside.

'This spot will do.' said the armed guard who spoke perfect English. He had said he was 'a bit of a shot' with the rifle he was carrying as we drove along in a remote area, the blue hills stretching away into the distance. The car stopped and we got out wondering quite what was coming next. Without a word, the guard went about seven paces away and built a small pile of stones. He returned to the car and started firing at the pile of stones. We were relieved on the one hand but, on the other, had to take rapid shelter as the ricochets and the odd stone came flying back. 'Now your turn!' We all had a go but no one aimed at the stones; we just fired away into the hills. We did not think he was a particularly good shot!

We went on, passing several forts, to see the Afghan border from the top of the hill. The few people we did see were all armed. We returned, stopping off at Landi Khotal, a thriving and busy market town but, more significantly, the place where all the local weapons are manufactured and sold.

Gilgit.
4,750 ft, 1,450 m.

Gilgit is the capital of the Hunza Valley, a valley made famous for its apricots which are laid out to dry on the flat roofs of many of the village houses. Gilgit was a northern outpost of the North West Frontier Region of British India. One tale of those times which appeals to me is of the District Officer, based in Gilgit, who, fed up with the local clerk who always reduced the mileage travelled by horse on the travel claim submitted by the DO to get to the head office in Peshawar, tore the milestone from the ground in Gilgit and placed it firmly on the clerk's desk.

From Peshawar, Jill, Tim, Sue and I bussed our way up the sometimes precipitous Karakoram highway, for once free of landslides. We made it safely to Gilgit. We spent three nights there, the administrative capital of the Hunza Valley, awakening each morning to the swirl of bagpipes, coming from the nearby Pakistan Army barracks. We hired a jeep and guide and, with the guide, bought cooking gear and food, mainly rice, from the busy market. With the vehicle fully laden, we jeeped northwards along the Highway for about fifteen miles, before turning off heading for the Naltar Valley to the West.

Naltar Valley.
About 12,000 ft, 3,650 m.

Having turned off the Highway, we continued along the track before it ran out in a small village where we hired a couple of donkeys and transferred our loads to them. We walked on through pine woods and passed lakes, with magical reflections of the surrounding mountains, before entering another village with, amazingly, a pasture and broad fields of ready-to-harvest wheat; the whole area was bathed in warm sunshine with the mountains forming a magnificent backdrop.

The village at about 11, 500 ft was sparsely populated and abandoned during the winter because of the snows; the inhabitants descending to their permanent homes at about 7,000 ft along the Highway. Such people as there were, of course, were all Moslem, associated with the Aga Khan. In such a heavenly place we were sorely tempted to accept their offer to build us a house there for two thousand pounds. But sleeping on it, the next day we realised that no foreigner, because he just might be able to afford it, had a right to butt in on their peaceful, if sometimes wild, haven. On recent reflection, given the troubles caused by the Taliban in that area, in any case, we made the right decision.

We continued our trek eventually reaching the snowline at about 12,000 ft where we camped just below it. Tim cooked supper that first night giving our cook a break; we played 'Book titles' around a blazing camp fire and then turned in.

There followed two days of very gentle walking the hills. On waking up on the last day we saw snow-leopard footprints near our tent. We retraced our tracks, giving up our donkeys once we reached our vehicle. It seemed a long journey to the Highway but we eventually reached it and returned to Gilgit.

Our guide and laden donkey.

Walking into the Naltar Valley.

A mountain reflected in the still lake.

One of our camp sites with the cook out hunting!

Harvests at 12000 ft.

The cook, Tim, Sue, with me and the guide.

Gulmit.
About 8,000 ft, 2,450 m.

After a leisurely start settling matters with our guide, we bussed from Gilgit to Gulmit, further North along the highway into Upper Hunza, Roughly halfway, some 5 miles from the road to the south lay the summit of Rakaposhi at 7786 m, 25,440 ft clearly visible from the road.

The whole journey required more than one bus because there were landslides and we had two punctures; it was dark when we arrived. We stayed in the Tourist Cottages which notably had hot water on tap. We spent two very pleasant days in the area, visiting the local museum, endeavouring, but failing, to walk to the head of the Passu Glacier and playing on a suspension bridge, across the Hunza river, a tributary of the Indus.

The suspension bridge, we thought, challenged us to cross it although we had no need. Jill, Tim and myself readily accepted the challenge, Sue also but reluctantly. The bridge appeared to be in disrepair but was definitely open – in more ways than one. Three pairs of wires stretched across to the distant bank; the top pair formed the handrails, the bottom two, all at the same level, carried the so-called deck which consisted of thin planks set every 40 or 50 centimetres or so but a lot of these planks were missing. We crossed with the muddy brown water moving southwards below us. Once across, we recrossed to our home bank. Sue confessed she was terrified; we three others did not do confessions.

The next day we waved Tim and Sue off. They travelled further North retracing our two-year old steps over the Khunjerab Pass to Kashgar and, thence, across China to Beijing; we would not hear from them for another three months. We waited by the roadside for a bus heading southward. We had been waiting for some time when the landlord of the Inn, where we had stayed the night, came out with a tray of tea for us which we drank thankfully, such kindness! Eventually the bus came and we journeyed, landslideless, to Peshawar where the next day we caught our plane home.

Crossing the Gulmit Bridge.

Nanga Parbat.
26,600 ft, 8,110 m.

It is perhaps relevant to reflect that climbing is not without its hazards but one could not make up the circumstances which led to the horrific deaths of so many people on this particular mountain. Although on our journey along the Karakoram Highway not far south of Gilgit, we do not recall actually seeing this notorious mountain, but we knew it lay no more than twelve miles to the South East of us.

Thirty-one people had died whilst attempting to climb this mountain before it was eventually summitted in 1953. This mountain therefore had, in those days, the reputation of being 'the killer mountain'. Since then, with over nine times more deaths on Everest that dubious title, with regard to the maximum number of deaths, has passed to the highest mountain itself. The second highest mountain, K2, records the highest ratio of deaths to attempts.[4] The prime cause of death, quite apart from altitude sickness, is generally an avalanche, with falls, exposure and other climbing hazards following. All these hazards are well known to climbers and, whilst accepting them, every attempt is made to minimise these risks. However, there was little the 11 climbers could do on Nanga Parbat in June 2013 when they were all killed at base camp by the Taliban. God rest all souls.

---

[4] The source for the statistics shown is the web and may be found by entering 'List of deaths on 8000 metre mountains' - Wikipedia. Under CC BY-SA Licence

1991. Everest Base Camp Trek, Nepal.

Lukla Airstrip.
9,195 ft, 2,803 m.

Lukla airstrip is generally regarded as the most dangerous in the world because of its altitude, rapidly changing weather conditions, short runway and location surrounded by mountains. With a conventional flight, the approach to the airfield is difficult and, once committed to a descent, there is no turning back. The pilot is required to enter a valley with mountains ahead and to left and right, a tight turn to starboard is required to align with the short, fortunately uphill, runway at the far end of which is the wall of a mountain. A helicopter landing is much easier.

Because of a late arrival in Kathmandu, Jill, Nick and I flew to Lukla in a helicopter which for us was exciting enough in itself. We were met by Tashi Tenzing who was to be our guide to take us to or near Everest base camp. Tashi is the grandson of Norgay Tenzing and a few years later he would follow his famous grandfather's footsteps to the summit of Everest but, in the meantime, he had to contend with us. No sooner was our kit unloaded than we were on our way to our first overnight stay in tents, en route towards Everest.

At the end of our two weeks in the Khumbu Valley, in a small conventional aircraft we would experience the short downhill take-off with the mountain on the other side of the valley quickly looming large ahead before the tight turn to port and the open skies.

The airstrip at Lukla.

Tashi Tenzing, grandson of Norgay,
our guide at Namche Bazaar.

Periche.
14,343 ft, 4,373 m.

En route to base camp is the small village of Periche. We camped for the night there when the overnight temperature dropped to -21 degrees Centigrade; everything was of course frozen solid and woe betide those who did not sleep with their boots inside their sleeping bag. The morning dawned, however, bright and sunny, just right for a walk in the surrounding hills, so I thought; despite it being a rest day to acclimatize.

I set off on my own and indeed did have a lovely walk for about four hours up a couple of hills. Naturally enough, this foolish virgin paid for it the next day on the walk to the village of Lobuche when the effects of altitude were felt; headache, cough and feeling weak. So much the latter that Jill kindly relieved me of my pack and carried it for me. When will I learn not to do stupid things and to acclimatize when advised?

Kala Patthar.
18,255 ft, 5565 m.

Gorak Shep, at 16,892 ft, (5,150m), is the last settlement before base camp; it was actually deserted and had been for some time. Beyond it is a level sandy area devoid of vegetation, a former lake bed; crossing that Jill and Nick went onto the slopes of Kala Pattar, a mountain immediately to the south west of base camp. Jill climbed to about 18,000 ft, (5,490 m). Nick who was climbing faster went on to the top. Jill waited for Nick, looking down on the base camp below, up at Everest itself, with its two guardians, Lhotse (27,932 ft, 8516 m), and Nuptse (25,784 ft, 7861 m), to its south and, more immediately ahead of her to the North, Pumori, (23,494 ft, 7,163 m).

With Jill and Nick on a cold start to the day at Periche.

On the top of Kala Patthar, Nick centre-rear with fellow climbers.

It was at nearly 20,000ft from the slopes of Pumori in 1951 that Shipton, accompanied by Hillary, determined that a route up Everest, formidable and challenging as it appeared, might 'go' via the South Col and would be worth trying. In the following few days, they found their way through the Khumbu icefall. Subsequently, when the British Ambassador in Kathmandu congratulated Hillary on finding a possible route up Everest, he told him almost in the same breath, that a Swiss expedition would take place the following year, prior to the British attempt in 1953. That news did not go down well but there was nought to be done except wait out, patiently, and prepare for the British attempt.[5]

Everest Base Camp, Nepal.
17,500 ft, 5,353 m.

The Nepalese Base Camp is situated in the Khumbu valley, some 15 miles roughly North East from the Tengboche Monastery, a glimpse of which Hillary and Tenzing saw below them on the morning they set off for the summit.[6] Just to the right of that line of sight, viewed from Tengboche, we saw another spectacular mountain, much closer to the monastery, Ama Dablam, at over 6,800 m (over 22,300 ft), traditionally called the Matterhorn of the Himalayas with a prominence of over 1000 metres. A wonderful sight!

Although Base Camp was first visited by Shipton and Hillary the year before them, it was, of course, the Swiss who first fully occupied it in 1952. Since that time the same area has been used many times by

---

[5] This paragraph is a paraphrase of information on pages 84 and 85 of Hillary's Account (^Ibid 1 refers).

[6] This paragraph is a paraphrase of information contained on page 12 of Hillary's Account (^Ibid 1 refers).

different nationalities. Reaching this is also an end in itself for many trekkers, including the Barker family, thousands visiting it each year.

For the 1953 British expedition, an advance party reached Base Camp some three weeks after leaving Banepa, approximately 15 miles East of Kathmandu, with the main body, involving some 800 porter loads, arriving four or five days later.[7] The walk-in itself contributed to climber's fitness and acclimitization. Nowadays, with the advent of the Lukla Airstrip, the long march from Kathmandu can be eliminated but, as I know to my cost, with the increased risk of altitude sickness.

---

[7] The information in this sentence is derived from pages 107 to 111 of Hillary's Account (^Ibid 1 refers).

2009. Land Rover Trip to Darjeeling, Gangtok (Sikkim) and Bhutan.

Darjeeling, India.
6042 ft, 2046 m.

In Darjeeling we stayed at the Windamere, It is the place to stay if you are nostalgic about England and, in 2009, wanted your tea, complete with scones, cream and jam served by uniformed maids wearing black with a little white pinafore. Although for speed we had arrived by Land Rover rather than the 'Toy Train', we could not resist the temptation to descend by train to a couple of stations and return the same way. The train journey is quite magical as it puffs its way, amid clouds of smoke and steam, though the bustling high street, preceded and followed by cars.

We stayed for two full days. The first morning we were up in the dark, well before breakfast, to watch, along with many Indian tourists, the wonderful sight of the sun rising over Kanchenjunga, the third highest mountain in the world.

When we got back to the hotel, we found a card in our room with a delightful poem, written years before by Jan Morris. The poem referred to Kanchenjunga, the Toy Train and the Windamere; whilst memories of the first two might fade, those of the Windamere never would.

We visited the Himalayan Mountaineering Institute built in 1954 to commemorate the success of Sherpa Norgay Tenzing in reaching the top of Everest. In the museum there, we were very excited to see, as an exhibit, the sleeping bag belonging to one of Jill's distant relatives, that of Noel Odell, a renowned climber of his day. We also read for the first time Edward Whymper's advice to climbers which is reproduced on the title page of this book.

155

On the road to Darjeeling – the Toy Train.

Early sunshine on Kanchenjunga.

Orchids at the entrance to the Hidden Forest Plant Research Station.

The Himalayan Mountaineering Institute.

Gangtok. Sikkim, India.
5510 ft, 1,650 m.

We visited Gangtok, the former capital of Sikkim, in October 2009. We stayed at the Hidden Forest, a plant research station, which had a close association with Kew Gardens. As one might imagine, the garden, full of orchids and other rare plants, provided a peaceful haven for us with a wonderfully clear view of Kanchenjunga in the distance on the Sikkim/Nepalese border. I sketched Jill as we relaxed in the garden.

Tiger's Nest Monastery and Temple, Bhutan.
10,232 ft, 3119 m.

We visited Bhutan straight after Sikkim. Bhutan is fascinating; everyone is required to wear national dress whilst at work and success is measured, not in term of GDP but, in happiness. Everyone was very friendly and welcoming. The only downside was that all foreigners were required to stay in designated hotels not used by the locals, so we seemed to meet more other nationals than we did Bhutanese. However Jill and I did a lot of independent walking in the hills, where we met lots of locals so that was good. We were intrigued by the mammoth phallic symbols which decorated most of the houses in the countryside, symbols of fertility warding off evil spirits.

Archery would appear to be their favourite sport and we were much impressed by the prowess we saw. We watched several competitions which were always joyful affairs; success at hitting the small target about 150 metres away was always followed by the archer, and sometimes his whole team, doing a little dance.

We visited many Buddhist temples which, for good reason in the old days, were more like little fortresses.

A typical house decoration in Bhutan especially in the countryside.

A competitor takes aim.

The main roads leading North in Bhutan were particularly good, built for obvious reason by India as aid to Bhutan, for quick access to the border up to which, on the other side, China had done the same where they had also apparently built hospitals.

One day we set off across the hills to walk to Tiger's Nest Monastery and temple, a dramatic building clinging to a vertical cliff face in the Paro Valley. After some hours walking, just as we thought we could not be too far away from the monastery, I became quite breathless, the altitude taking its due effect on me. I stopped where I was whilst Jill went on alone. She got within 250 metres from the monastery but it was across a deep, steep sided valley, the path descending nearly to the valley floor and up the other side. However, worried about me and at least having seen the monastery close to, she turned back and re-joined me. We walked back slowly.

The Tiger's Nest Monastery.

Silhouette of Jill as she comes round the mountain.

2020-21. Everest, Including by the Stairs, and Other High Mountains.

New Height of Everest.
29,031.69 ft, 8848.86 m.

On December 2020, just as I had reached a quarter the way up Everest on the stairs, it was jointly announced by Nepal and China that a recent survey had shown that the mountain was 86 cm higher than when first measured. Just my luck! I hoped that this addition would not prove to be the last straw that broke the camel's back.

Tibetan Base Camp.
About 16,900 ft, 5,150 m.

With Mount Everest lying on the border between Tibet and Nepal and, at that time, Nepal closed to visitors, the first attempts to climb Everest were made from the Tibetan side, in 1921 and by the British. The aim of the 1921 expedition was to determine a suitable approach to the foot of the mountain and site a base camp. This they did selecting a site in the East Rongbuk Glacier valley, several miles South of Rongbuk monastery. They would tackle the mountain via the North Col. Base camps for the subsequent British expeditions in 1922 and 1924 were all sited in the same valley.

The approach march starting in Kathmandu was much longer than that for the Nepalese camp, taking for the 1924 expedition, with its 800 porter loads and involving 200 yaks, some 36 days.[8]

---

[8]The approach march with timings is described from pages 18 to 42 of Norton's account (^Ibid 2). Yaks were not the only transport animals; as set out at page 36, for 6 days of the march donkeys were used. They carry the same load of about 160 lbs and travel faster than yaks.

The 1922 expedition reached a height of about 27,320ft before disaster struck with the loss of 7 porters in an avalanche.[9] The attempt in 1924 resulted in the disappearance of Mallory and Irvine; Odell played a significant part in that expedition.

Nowadays, following the Chinese takeover of Tibet and Nepal open, most attempts are made from the Nepalese side. In 1951, however, despite starting from the Nepalese side and the presence of Chinese soldiers at the Rongbuk Monastery, the Tibetan base site was nevertheless visited by Hillary and his compatriot George Lowe. After overcoming substantial climbing difficulties, they crossed a pass, the Nup La at 19,400 ft, on the Nepal/Tibet border and spent five days in the valley. They found a route through the East Rongbuk glacier icefall before returning to Nepal via the same pass.[10]

Khumbu Icefall.
About 19,500 ft, 6,000 m.

The front face of the icefall is close to base camp and the approximate height above is at the higher end of the fall. The icefall, by its very name, is moving and as such constitutes the most dangerous part of the climb.

Apart from avalanche and falling ice blocks (some massive), there are crevasses to cross. Some of these can be stepped across, others descended into and up the other side and yet others crossed on snow bridges or by using equipment bridges.

---

[9] The height reached and the loss of porters is indicated in the web by entering 1922 British Everest Expedition 1922 – Wikipedia. Attributed to The Geographical Journal No 2

[10] The sentences starting with 'In 1951, however, despite ....' and ending with '... via the same pass.' is a paraphrase of the information contained in pages 91 to 95 of Hillary's Account (^Ibid 1 refers).

Fortunately, no such hazards bar my stair climb but, in a card this Christmas, Phil Neame (he of Lamjung who joined two subsequent Everest expeditions) warned me to watch out 'for total collapse of the stairs' during this phase of my climb.

Mount Kailash, Tibet.
21,773 ft, 6638 m.

This mountain, situated just North of the Indian border in Tibet, is not strictly in the Himalayan range but it is within just a few miles of it and is included here because it is my favourite mountain. It has fascinated me for years. It is the holiest of mountains for four religions including Hinduism and Buddhism; many pilgrims have circumnavigated the mountain on their kora and it remains, and I hope always will, unclimbed. Whether pilgrims are permitted to enter China nowadays to pay homage to the mountain is another matter.

Mount Kailash forms part of the Gangdesi range which lies in a relatively small area which contains the sources of three great rivers. The Indus flows initially westwards before turning South to empty into the Arabian sea, almost two thousand miles away; the Ganges flows initially southwards, before turning westwards to enter the Bay of Bengal some 1600 miles downstream and the source of the Brahmaputra, which also flows into the same Bay, is in the same Mount Kailash area nearly 2,500 miles upstream.

---

[11] The photo of Mount Kailash is attributed to Ondrej Zvacak. CC BY-SA 3.0 via Wikimedia Commons and may readily be seen on the web by entering
http://commons.wikimedia.org/wiki/file.kailash_north.jpg
No change made to the photo.

Mount Kailash, a mountain considered holy by 4 religions, including Hinduism and Buddhism.[1]

Life beyond 23,000 ft. Acclimatization and Use of Oxygen.
About 23,000 ft, 7,000 m.

Only two years prior to the 1924 expedition it was being debated whether life could be sustained above 25,000 ft without the use of oxygen.[12a] The 1924 expedition settled that debate with Odell playing a significant role in this matter. He remained at high altitude, mainly on his own, for twelve days, climbing to Camp 6 at 26,800 ft on a couple of occasions, but generally sleeping at a lower altitude but always, except for one night, at or above 23,000 ft,[12b] Odell only occasionally used oxygen and he considered that it gave him only minimal support which rarely outweighed the encumbrance of the equipment.[12c] In other words, Odell showed that slow acclimatisation was the secret of success.[12d] It was also found that those who had climbed to such heights before the expedition were better acclimatised than those who were experiencing such altitudes for the first time.[12e] As is well known, Everest has been climbed without the use of oxygen but it is perhaps best to have a supply to hand - just in case of an emergency.[12f]

However, above a certain height, now considered to be about 26,000 ft, one's body might still be able to acclimatise but it loses weight, strength and becomes listless, only the spirit of the individual driving him or her on. That height is dramatically, but justifiably, known today as the start of the 'death zone'.

---

[12]This paragraph is a paraphrase of information given on pages 87 for note a; page 114 for b; Pages 260 and 261 for c; page 261 for d; page155 for e and page 258 for f, all from Norton's Account (^Ibid 2 refers).

Nanda Devi, India.
25,643 ft, 7,818 m.

This mountain, which is the highest mountain to be wholly located within India, is another which Jill and I have never even seen but has to be included because it was first climbed by Jill's relative, Noel Odell.

The mountain has two summits, the western one being the highest. The mountain is particularly steep sided and difficult to access, a circle of high mountains surrounds it. A route across these mountains, into the Nanda Devi sanctuary, was reconnoitred by various explorers for many years before, in 1934, Eric Shipton and Bill Tilman found a way through the Rishi Gorge, a deep narrow canyon. Two years later, Tilman returned with Noel Odell and together they reached the top, at the time until after the second World War, the highest summit ever climbed.[13]

It is interesting to note that Norgay Tenzing, as a member of a French expedition, was one of the first to climb Nanda Devi East, two years before he reached the summit of Everest.[14]

1924. Odell has the last sighting of Mallory and Irving.
About 26,100 ft, 7,960 m.

Odell was the last to sight Mallory and Irvine before they disappeared. He himself describes the sighting in the definitive account of the 1924

---

[13]This paragraph is a paraphrase of information about Nanda Devi contained in the web and may be found by entering 'Nanda Devi – Wikipedia'. Wikipedia under CC BY-SA Licence. Andy Fanshawe & Stephen Venables 'Himalaya Alpine Style' Hodder & Stoughton 1993 and Tilman HW 'The Ascent of Nanda Devi' Cambridge University Press 1937.

[14]This paragraph is a paraphrase of information taken from the web and may be found by entering 'Everest Today 'Norgay Tenzing's Road to the Summit of Everest, a Blog by Chhabri Pokhrel dated 31 July 2020. This entry also shows that Tenzing, starting in 1935, took part in five earlier attempts to climb Everest before his eventual success.

expedition published the following year. His description is reproduced below:

"At about 26,000ft I climbed a little crag which could possibly have been circumvented, but which I decided to tackle direct, more as a test of my condition than for any other reason. There was scarcely 100 ft of it, and as I reached the top there was a sudden clearing of the atmosphere above me and I saw the whole summit ridge and final peak of Everest unveiled. I noticed far away on a snow slope leading up to what seemed to me to be the last step but one from the base of the final pyramid, a tiny object moving and approaching the rock step. A second object followed, and then the first climbed to the top of the step. As I stood intently watching this dramatic appearance, the scene became enveloped in cloud once more, and I could not actually be certain that I saw the second figure join the first. It was of course, none other than Mallory and Irvine."[15]

Highest Point climbed by man prior to 1953 Everest expedition. *28,000 ft, 8,540 m.*

28,126 ft was the highest recorded height man had ever climbed on any expedition prior to the successful ascent of Everest in 1953. This feat was first achieved by Norton, the leader of the 1924 British expedition via the North Col route.[16]

Norgay Tenzing himself and Lambert, a Swiss climber, also reached near that height on the 1952 Swiss attempt via the South Col. Utterly exhausted, they had gone as far as they could go after a miserable night,

---

[15] This extract, written by Odell, is taken from page 102 in Norton's Account (^Ibid 2 refers).

[16] The height was later measured by theodolite as indicated at page 90 of Norton's Account (^Ibid 2 refers).

without sleeping bags or food in the camp they had established with two others at about 27,500 ft. They retreated, the end of the Swiss attempt.[17]

Kanchenjunga, India.
28,169 ft, 8,58 m.

As recorded earlier, this mountain was viewed by Jill and me from Darjeeling and later, Gangtok. It was first climbed in 1955 by Joe Brown and George Band. As the story goes, out of respect for the local population who considered the mountain sacred, they stopped short, a matter of feet, from the summit itself.[18]

K2, Pakistan.
28,251 ft, 8611 m.

This mountain is included for two reasons. The first is to acknowledge the success of the ten Sherpas who made the first winter ascent of this notoriously difficult mountain; a radio announcement about their success was made on 16 January 2021 whilst I was still plodding my way up my stairs. The second, and for me more important, reason is to stress its significance. To me, they represent all Sherpas upon whom so many other climbers have necessarily relied to enable them to reach other summits.

---

[17] This paragraph 'Norgay Tenzing himself.....the Swiss attempt' is derived from the information at Page 96 of Hillary's Account (^Ibid 1 refers).

[18] The sentence which includes '...out of respect.... itself' is derived from the web and may be found by entering 1955 British Kanchenjunga Expedition – Wikipedia. Under CC BY-SA Licence Evans Charles (1956) 'Kanchenjunga, The Untrodden Peak' Hodder and Stoughton.

Hillary Step.
28,839 ft, 8792 m.

This 'step', reached on the South Col route, is the 40 ft wall some 200ft below the summit of Everest. The step presented Hillary and Tenzing with their greatest challenge on the day they reached the top. More recently, with fixed ropes, the step has often become the bottleneck for the many climbers who have since summited, sometimes having to queue for the opportunity to climb it.

Summit of Everest.
29, 031.69 ft, 8848.86 m.

Jill and Nick had great views of the summit of Everest from Kala Patthar. Jill, in particular, thought about Mallory and Irvine, wondering if they got to the top, and of her relative Odell on the same expedition. She also recalled the excitement of the day when news of Hillary's and Tenzing's success reached England. There was in any case much to celebrate on that day, the Queen's Coronation and watching the ceremony on a television set up in the church, although the planned street-party had to be curtailed because it was too cold to linger outside.

My little success in reaching my 'Everest' summit on 24 February 2021 after 'climbing' 3,416 flights of stairs (44,408 steps) was not so exciting. Nevertheless, we did celebrate it with a bottle of champagne - and because it was Jill's birthday!

Mount Everest – The view from Kala Patthar.

Reaching my 'Everest' summit
after 3,416 flights of stairs.

Yesterdays upon the Stairs

Final Thoughts

Whilst Hillary and Tenzing were the first recorded people to reach the summit, I like to think that Mallory and Irvine, 29 years earlier, reached the summit but were not allowed to return, in the same way as over 300 other people were subsequently not allowed.

Without doubt, climbing Everest, or indeed any mountain, is a self-indulgent pastime. I confess, however, had I been offered the opportunity to join an expedition to climb it, and not pay money for the privilege, I would have jumped at the chance. Nevertheless, given my susceptibility to altitude sickness I doubt I would have got very far.

For me on the stairs for a period of 15 weeks, that too was self-indulgence but it did give me time to recall other mountains and places with which Jill and I, or family, had been associated. At the very least it kept me off the streets during lockdown. I now feel as fit as Nick and Tim - well, almost!

Yesterdays upon the Stairs

Mountains/Events by Height

10 ft	3 m	Upstairs Window, Mill House, England
10 ft	3 m	Shamshui Po, Hong Kong
72 ft	22 m	Cranbrook Mill, England
75 ft	23 m	Cranbrook Church Tower, England
400 ft	122 m	Point Wild, Elephant Island, Antarctica
561 ft	171 m	Montana Roja, Tenerife, Spain
800 ft	250 m	Cape Wrath, Scotland.
900 ft	275 m	Balloon Ride, Kent, England
1,000 ft	300 m	A Hill, near Trough of Bowland, England
1,000 ft	305 m	Parachuting Height, Bardufoss, Norway
1,060 ft	323 m	Peshawar, Pakistan. Naltar Trek
1,261 ft	385 m	Helm Crag, Lake District, England
2,010 ft	612 m	'The Edge of the World', Riyadh, Saudi Arabia
2,100 ft	640 m	Slopes of Sunset Peak, Lantau Island, Hong Kong
2,545 ft	776 m	Mada'in Salih, Saudi Arabia
2,635 ft	803 m	Coniston Old Man, Lake District England
2,739 ft	835 m	The Pools of Dee, Larig Ghru, Scotland
2,759 ft	841 m	St Sunday Crag, Lake District, England
2,904 ft	885 m	Wli Falls, Volta Region, Ghana
2,906 ft	886 m	Pen y Fan, Wales
3,000 ft	915 m	Pokhara, Nepal
3,053 ft	931 m	Skiddaw, Cumbria
3,100 ft	945 m	The Heaney Glacier, South Georgia Island
3,116 ft	950 m	Thompson's Falls, Kenya
3,116 ft	950 m	Helvellyn, Lake District, England
3,208 ft	978 m	Scafell Pike, Lake District, England
3,610 ft	1,100 m	Khyber Pass, Pakistan

3,734 ft 1,138 m Dunhuang, China
3,742 ft 1,141 m Cairngorm, Scotland.
4,170 ft 1,271 m Kashgar, West China.
4,493 ft 1,370 m Ben Nevis, Scotland.
4,500 ft 1,372 m Kathmandu, Nepal.
4,750 ft 1,450 m Tatopani, Tilicho
4,750 ft 1,450 m Gilgit, Baltistan, Pakistan.
4,777 ft 1,456 m Fraser's Hill, Malaysia
5,410 ft 1,650 m Gangtok, Sikkim, India
6,500 ft 1,980 m Jangekot, Nepal
6,625 ft 2,020 m Ulleri, Nepal
6,710 ft 2,046 m Darjeeling, India
7,200 ft 2,200 m Horten's Plain, Sri Lanka
8,000 ft 2 450 m Forest Camp, Lamjung, Nepal.
8,000 ft 2,450 m Gulmit, Baltistan, Pakistan
8,154 ft 2,486 m Ootacomund, India
8,410 ft 2,564 m Yellowstone National Park, Wyoming, USA
8,833 ft 2,693 m Huayna Picchu, Peru
8,850 ft 2,700 m Marpha, Nepal
9,000 ft 2,750 m Meadow/Shelter, Nepal
9,000 ft 2,750 m Johmsom, Nepal
9,195 ft 2,803 m Lukla Airstrip, Nepal
9,216 ft 2,810 m Golmud, China
10,232 ft 3,119 m Tiger's Nest Monastery, Bhutan
11,946 ft 3,642 m La Paz, Bolivia
12,000 ft 3,650 m Naltar Valley, Pakistan
12,000 ft 3,650 m Lhasa, Tibet
12,000 ft 3,650 m Boulder Caves, Nepal
12,188 ft 3,715 m Mount Teide, Tenerife, Spain
12,507 ft 3,812 m Lake Titicaca, Peru
13,000 ft 3,950 m Tilicho Base Camp, Nepal
13,000 ft 3,950 m Lamjung Pre-Base Camp, Nepal

13,500 ft 4,100 m Lamjung Base Camp, Nepal
13,600 ft 4,150 m Two miles South of Base Camp, Lamjung
14,343 ft 4,373 m Periche, Nepal
15,450 ft 4,710 m Khunjerab Pass, China
15,500 ft 4,725 m Advanced Base, Lamjung, Nepal
15,770 ft 4,808 m Mont Blanc, French/Italian Border
15,988 ft 4,873 m La Marmotte. (Height climbed on bicycle)
16,000 ft 4,900 m Mountain Passes in Tibet
16,100 ft 4,910 m Lake Tilicho, Nepal
16,900 ft 5,150 m Everest Base Camp, Tibet
17,500 ft 5,335 m Everest Base Camp, Nepal
17,800 ft 5,270 m Camp 1, Lamjung, Nepal
18,000 ft 5,490 m Mount 'High Life', Nepal
18,255 ft 5,565 m Kala Patthar, Nepal
18,900 ft 5,750 m Snowhole, Lamjung, Nepal
19,342 ft 5,895 m Kilimanjaro, Tanzania
19,500 ft 6,000 m Khumbu Icefall, Nepal
19,800 ft 6,036 m Camp 2, Lamjung, Nepal
21,500 ft.6,555 m Camp 3, Lamjung, Nepal
21,773 ft 6,638 m Mount Kailash, Tibet
22,911 ft 6,983 m The Summit, Lamjung, Nepal
23,000 ft 7,000 m Life beyond 23,000 feet
23,500 ft 7,160 m Air Reconnaissance
25,643 ft 7,818 m Nanda Devi, India
26,100 ft 7,960 m Odell's Last Sight of Mallory & Irvine
26,600 ft 8,110 m Nanga Parbat, Pakistan
28,000 ft 8,540 m Highest Point climbed prior to 1953
28,169 ft 8,588 m Kanchenjunga, India
28,251 ft 8,611 m K2, Pakistan
28,839 ft 8,792 m Hillary Step, Everest, Nepal
29, 031.69 ft 8,848.86 m The Summit, Everest